50 DOs for Everyday Leadership

Dear Miss Rolf,
    Thank you for being a
wonderful first grade
teacher! We appreciate
your patience, care and
Christian example for
the children and for us.

        Blessings in
        your everyday
        leadership,

            Lynn Townsend

— Career Day 2008 —

50 DOs for Everyday Leadership:

Practical Lessons Learned the Hard Way
(So You Don't Have To)

John Barrett
David Wheatley
Lynn Townsend

Foreword by
Denis Ives

Humanergy®
213 West Mansion Street
Marshall, MI 49068

Library of Congress Control Number: 2006940434

ISBN 978-0-9772062-0-9

Printed and bound by Sheridan Books
Cover design by Desktop Miracles

HUMANERGY®, the HUMANERGY® logo, DESIRED™, FACET™, ICUC™, TrueSuccess™, and BrainBuilding™ are trademarks of HUMANERGY®, Inc., Marshall, Michigan. For information, contact HUMANERGY® at 213 West Mansion Street, Marshall, MI 49068 / 269.789.0446 / e-mail info@humanergy.com / web www.humanergy.com or www.50DOs.com

This publication is designed to provide accurate and authoritative information in regard to the subject matter covered. It is sold with the understanding that neither the author nor the publisher is engaged in rendering legal, accounting, or other professional service. If legal advice or other expert assistance is required, the services of a competent professional person should be sought.
-From a Declaration of Principles jointly adopted by a Committee of the American Bar Association and a Committee of Publishers.

For Our Families

Acknowledgments

Many thanks and warm appreciation to the following people who contributed their time and talents to the *50 DOs for Everyday Leadership* book project: Rick Barnett, Pat Barrett, Paula Bokoch, Dan DiSebastian, Maurice Evans, Denis Ives, Bill Jefferson, Leigh Johnson, Kyle Keller, Jennifer McEldowney, Dan Ohmer, Laura Oliver, Ron Owens, Karen Parker, Stephanie Pierce, Jossie Prochilo, Gary Shelton, Bob Slocum, Angela Wheatley, Ernest Wheatley and Becky Zona. Special thanks to our editor-in-chief, Christi Barrett.

We also wish to thank our clients who have affirmed the *50 DOs for Everyday Leadership* over the past six years.

A special thanks to our families for supporting us in our core values, which include making a real difference in the world by "improving the lives of the individuals we work with and thus the people and organizations they touch."

Foreword

Leadership has many facets and, inevitably, many books have emerged to address them. Readers with an active interest in the lexicon of leadership will be well aware of those volumes that seek to deal with issues of vision, mission and strategy. Many such books are becoming more complex, less user friendly and heavier in theory than seems necessary.

50 DOs for Everyday Leadership: Practical Lessons Learned the Hard Way (So You Don't Have To) is unique in its scope, focus and size. It is not theoretical, but based on experiential learning. And although it recognizes the contextual importance of higher-level issues like vision, mission and strategy, it is essentially about practical and tactical issues of the workplace—building and maintaining relationships with fellow employees, which provide the underpinnings of sound and effective leadership.

As the title suggests, the book discusses 50 leadership topics grouped under seven practical questions encompassing good practice, common sense, improved processes and sensible behaviours. In each instance it sets out what good leaders do and cautions about the things that they shouldn't do. Moreover, it discusses attitudes, difficulties, potential rewards and useful connections between specific topics, creating a fabric of interconnections among sections.

We have to be aware of how behaviours and practices work through the eyes of a leader and through the eyes of a follower—we may frequently encounter this challenge in the space of a single working day. Then, both leaders and followers can use this book in various ways depending upon their roles in the organization.

For those who have been in leadership roles for some time, this book can serve as a valuable refresher and reminder about key behaviours. For those new to leadership roles, or those aspiring to such roles in terms of career advancement, it is a timely and reliable guide for the behaviours necessary for success.

For some these behaviours may prove relatively easy. For others it may be more challenging, and the suggestions in this book may have to be revisited a number of times. Good leadership, however, is not formulaic, but must demonstrate a natural credibility based on repeated good practice.

This book will appeal to those who want to develop and follow a reflective and intelligent style of leadership, based on good practice and improved relationships in the workplace. I commend the leadership team at Humanergy® for the time and effort they have put into this practical and informative guide to improved leadership in the workplace.

Denis Ives
October 2006

Denis Ives was the Public Service Commissioner for the Australian Public Service (APS) from 1990 to 1995 and is now an independent management consultant, located in Canberra, Australia. During his term as Commissioner, Mr. Ives advised the Australian Government on major public service reform and leadership and management issues. Prior to becoming Public Service Commissioner, Mr. Ives had a wide ranging career in government service, including extensive involvement in major industry and resource developments. In 1997, he was made an Officer of the Order of Australia (AO) for services to government and industry.

*Management is doing things right;
leadership is doing the right things.*
Peter F. Drucker
Author, professor & management consultant

Contents

INTRODUCTION
Why 50 DOs & DON'Ts?

Picture this…you are a news reporter geared up to interview frontline supervisors. Your mission is to gather as much leadership advice as you can. Your goal is to write a simple, straightforward piece on leadership: how it's done, day in, day out.

Throughout the day you talk to small groups of supervisors. In total their experience and leadership lessons are almost greater than the number of books in the Library of Congress. As they talk you write furiously to capture the successes and failures. You pay particular attention to their wisdom. You are drawn by their voices—the authentic, down-to-earth practical advice. "This is great," you say to yourself, "I wish I had known this stuff long before today!"

That's just about what happened. Humanergy's co-founders, John Barrett and David Wheatley, interviewed one hundred veteran, frontline supervisors and asked them two questions:

"What are the basic rules to survive as a leader?"
"What advice would you give to a new leader?"

Capturing the advice verbatim, the result was a list of 150 leadership rules. The list was then distilled to 50 DOs and DON'Ts. *50 DOs for Everyday Leadership* reflects these core essentials to practical leadership—the key attitudes and actions.

 The DOs are something you should start or keep doing (like a green light). The DON'Ts are something you should stop or not start (like a red light).

In the six years that have followed these interviews, thousands of leaders have validated their practicality and credibility—that the most successful leaders do the DOs and avoid the DON'Ts.

Who should read this book?

50 DOs for Everyday Leadership is a practical leadership guide and reference. The DOs and DON'Ts are for new leaders, employees transitioning into leadership roles, leaders who never got the leadership training and advice they needed, and leaders who want a practical refresher in successful leadership behaviors. People who aspire to leadership roles will use this book to understand what it takes to be a leader.

Read and share this book if one or more of these statements apply to YOU:

- "I'm not a leader yet, but I want to be."

- "I'm good at what I do, so they are putting me in charge of people and increasing my responsibilities."

- "I've been a leader for a while, but never got any (or enough) leadership training and coaching."

- "I'm a leader, and I need a 'back-to-basics' refresher."

- "My boss gave me this book and told me to read it."

You learn something every day
if you pay attention.
Ray LeBlond
Director of Communications, British Columbia

Using this Book

50 DOs for Everyday Leadership is like having a personal leadership coach with you in the trenches. The practical ideas for each DO represent more than a quarter-century of leadership coaching advice and experience.

Consider this book your *field guide*—a tool to help you be more successful and ignite the success of the people and organizations you influence each day.

For every DO there is a DON'T. Each *pair* should be read together to understand its context i.e., the leadership situations where it applies.

And each pair is tied to one of *seven key leadership questions* that are also the chapter headings:

- How do I build trust and credibility?

- How do I get my people working together as a team?

- How do I keep perspective on what's important?

- How do I make sure people get things done?

- How do I do what's best for the organization?

- How do I reduce misunderstandings and get people on the same page?

- How do I continue to improve what my people and I are doing?

As you read, digest, ponder and use this guide, here are four suggestions to help you personalize, maximize and discipline your success:

    A. Read the book from front to back and pick areas that apply to you, then share the book with your team.

    B. Do the self-assessment on pages 9-10 and focus initially on one strength and one area to improve.

    C. Use the 50 DOs worksheet on page 13 to plan for performance reviews, one-on-one coaching and meetings and to summarize lessons learned at the end of a project.

    D. Keep this book as a reference when you need quick leadership advice.

The following pages guide you through the process of implementing one or more of these four suggestions.

A. Read the book from front to back and pick areas that apply to you, then share the book with your team.

As you read highlight the advice that rings true to you—take notes in the margins and tab with sticky notes.

Add "Your Success" tips on the lines provided. Highlight the "Connected DOs" to help you jumpstart your progress.

Then, LIVE THE DOs!

Model your leadership choices with an attitude of *continuous* and *contagious* personal improvement.

Next, to maximize the results, share this book with your team. Use the following small group exercise to boost your *team's success*:

- Give a copy of the book to each team member.

- Ask your team to review the book and highlight what they learned, as well as what surprised them.

- Schedule a one-hour meeting with your entire team to discuss their DO strengths and challenges and come up with the beginning of an improvement plan.

- Explain in advance the meeting's expectations and outcomes.

- Share specific points from the book that really impacted you and your choices as a leader; explain your commitment to being a great leader and the area(s) you are ready to improve.

- Divide into pairs; take 30 minutes to discuss two or three key points where each person wants to improve performance.

- Ask each person to individually reflect for ten minutes how she will implement a change in the next month; use the FACET™ tool on page 63 to provide the framework for making the change.

- Ask each person to tell the team the change he would like to make and the FACET™ steps to get there.

When you see successes in the next month, acknowledge them! Likewise, if your team is slipping back into negative habits, point it out firmly, but sensitively.

B. Do the self-assessment and focus initially on one strength and one area to improve.

Complete pages 9-10. Pick a DO in which you are successful. Also, pick a DON'T that needs improvement—one that challenges you, yet isn't too hard to improve. (For a downloadable Self-Assessment worksheet, visit www.humanergy.com.)

For the DO you do well, read the related DO page tips and pick one or two ideas to continue your path of success. For the DON'T that needs improvement, choose one or two ideas to help you manage it.

Here's an example: A successful DO for you is *DO 16—Solicit ideas from others to shape decisions.* You will start asking each team member to come to a meeting prepared with two possible solutions to a pressing problem.

A DON'T where you need to improve is *DON'T 22—Let disruptive people have an audience.* You will start using meeting best practices to minimize conflict up front. And, you'll practice the phrase "I see you are upset..." to calm an employee who is frustrated.

To help you achieve the results you want, use the FACET™ tool on page 63. The following page shows what your FACET™ might look like.

FACET™ Example

- FOCUS: DO 22—Defuse situations and deal with people one-on-one.

- ACCOUNTABILITY: Ask James and Raakesh to check your progress once a week.

- CONSEQUENCES: When you successfully manage one-on-one interactions for one week, reward yourself with an extra round of weekend golf. However if you lose control of your staff meeting, penalize yourself by not playing any golf for one week.

- EASIER TO DO: Use a meeting facilitator to minimize conflict up front, focus the discussion and keep meetings on topic.

- TRACKING: Keep a daily tally of your progress in your planner.

50 DOs Self-Assessment

The DOs that I do well:

DO   **Page**

50 DOs Self-Assessment

The DON'Ts that I can improve:

DON'T   **Page**

_____

_____

_____

_____

_____

_____

_____

_____

_____

_____

C. Use the 50 DOs Worksheet to plan performance reviews, one-on-one coaching and meetings and to summarize lessons learned at the end of a project.

Fill in the worksheet on page 13 when you are preparing for a performance review, coaching session or meeting and pulling together lessons learned when a project ends. (You can download a copy of the 50 DOs worksheet at www.humanergy.com.)

For performance reviews and one-on-one coaching sessions, share with an employee what DOs you think she does well and the ones she can improve.

For improvement areas, use the 50 DOs worksheet to describe the issue/opportunity and the DOs that apply. Create an action plan with her, including a follow-up session to review progress and decide the next steps.

The following table is an example of a 50 DOs worksheet action plan.

What is the issue or opportunity?	Which DO(s) apply?
Earlene doesn't speak up in meetings and share her ideas; she has a hard time being assertive and difficulty admitting when she's used poor judgment.	30 Face up to issues and deal with them.
	4 Do what's right—stick to decisions or admit mistakes.
	31 Fight for doing the right thing—if you know about it, you are responsible for it.
What is my action plan?	
Share one idea in weekly team meetings; Pedro will remind me.	
Apologize when I make a mistake; Karen will remind me.	
Schedule a meeting with Yuri and Kim to discuss the overtime issue.	

For meetings:

- Before the meeting use the worksheet and decide what DOs apply to each agenda item.

- During the meeting share your pre-work with your team.

- Then create action steps to address each issue.

For lessons learned at the end of a project:

- Write a lesson learned in the "What is the issue or opportunity?" box.

- Choose which DOs apply.

- Use the action plan for future projects to decide how your team will repeat what went well and avoid what didn't work.

50 DOs Worksheet

Copy and use this worksheet to plan for performance reviews, one-on-one coaching and meetings and to summarize lessons learned at the end of a project (download at www.humanergy.com).

What is the issue or opportunity?	Which DO(s) apply?

What is my action plan?

How did I do?	What are my next steps?

© Humanergy, Inc.   269.789.0446   www.humanergy.com

D. Keep this book as a reference when you need quick leadership advice.

When you need leadership advice, use the seven leadership questions (the chapter headings) to guide you to the appropriate DOs that link to your specific leadership challenge. Then read the tips on those DO pages to get you started.

- **How do I build trust and credibility?**
  (DOs 1 - 8 starting on page 22)

- **How do I get my people working together as a team?**
  (DOs 9 - 17 starting on page 44)

- **How do I keep perspective on what's important?**
  (DOs 18 - 23 starting on page 72)

- **How do I make sure people get things done?**
  (DOs 24 - 29 starting on page 88)

- **How do I do what's best for the organization?**
  (DOs 30 - 35 starting on page 104)

- **How do I reduce misunderstandings and get people on the same page?**
  (DOs 36 - 41 starting on page 120)

- **How do I continue to improve what my people and I are doing?**
  (DOs 42 - 50 starting on page 142)

50 DOs List

How do I build trust and credibility?	
DO	DON'T
1. Be consistently 100% honest	1. Use half-truths, spin or avoid
2. Say "I don't know; I'll find out"	2. Pretend to be someone you're not
3. Lead by example – hold yourself to a higher standard	3. Say one thing and do another
4. Do what's right – stick to decisions or admit mistakes	4. Cut deals with people or be a pushover
5. Commit to the extent of your knowledge and authority	5. Overcommit to things outside your control
6. Make decisions when you need to	6. Freeze and get overrun
7. Circle back to interested parties – with follow-up, feedback, information or an answer	7. Leave people wondering
8. Maintain confidences and trust of those who are absent	8. Break confidences or talk behind people's backs

50 DOs List

How do I get my people working together as a team?

DO	DON'T
9. Trust people and check their work when necessary	9. Let people chase you away
10. Learn people's first names and greet everyone, every day, as a priority	10. Wait until making assignments to interact with people
11. Know who your people are, their qualifications, jobs and where they're located	11. Be unaware of who your people are
12. Get to know your people on a personal level	12. Be buddies or a stranger
13. Spend time side-by-side with people	13. Spend all your time in your office
14. Treat people with respect and tell them when they've done a good job	14. Treat people like they're idiots
15. Give out work assignments, document accountability and hold people accountable	15. Duck responsibility for ensuring work gets done and hope it works out
16. Solicit ideas from others to shape decisions	16. Shut people down
17. Set expectations and boundaries for jobs and provide necessary information	17. Tell people "just do it" or how to do it

50 DOs List

How do I keep perspective on what's important?	
DO	DON'T
18. Stay open-minded when receiving feedback	18. Make or take it personally
19. Ask for help	19. Try and do it by yourself
20. Choose your own behavior, demonstrate a positive attitude and work to influence others	20. React to other people and let them push your buttons
21. Focus your efforts – pick your issues and your time	21. React to everything and lose your focus
22. Defuse situations and deal with people one-on-one	22. Let disruptive people have an audience
23. Focus on the issue and not the person: "I'm not mad at you, but this behavior is unacceptable because…"	23. Make conflict personal and emotional

50 DOs List

How do I make sure people get things done?	
DO	DON'T
24. Step into a job with intensity for success – do what you can to make things better	24. Wait for someone else to do something
25. Collect the information needed for any given task from your people	25. Gloss over necessary details
26. Insist on accountability and potential solutions for problems, then help with the right things	26. Do people's jobs for them
27. Be consistent with expectations, but adjust approach to the individual	27. Work from one size fits all or be inconsistent
28. Write down thoughts, facts and issues – make lists, prioritize and check off	28. Operate without taking notes – rely on memory
29. Prepare and start the day with a game plan – to dos	29. Begin each day with no forethought or preparation

50 DOs List

How do I do what's best for the organization?

DO	DON'T
30. Face up to issues and deal with them	30. Walk away and avoid issues
31. Fight for doing the right thing – if you know about it, you are responsible for it	31. Keep your mouth shut
32. Put the organization and its people first	32. Put yourself first, "not my problem, not my job"
33. Accept "this is our assignment" and work to make it succeed	33. Say "I don't agree with this, but I've been told we have to do it"
34. Get the right people involved and on the same page	34. Make all the decisions and define all necessary actions
35. Work with key stakeholders and other resources (e.g., departments, people)	35. Operate in a silo

50 DOs List

How do I reduce misunderstandings and get people on the same page?	
DO	DON'T
36. Work through issues <u>with</u> people; listen first, then discuss	36. Use authority first or too quickly
37. Explain why or how decisions are made	37. Say "I don't want to hear it; just do it"
38. Listen and understand first, then act	38. Make snap judgments
39. Repeat back a summary of what people have told you	39. Assume mutual understanding
40. Be completely clear about your follow-up – what you will do and won't do	40. Create false expectations because you weren't clear
41. Start meetings with rules and boundaries for discussion	41. Let discussions get out of control

50 DOs List

How do I continue to improve what my people and I are doing?	
DO	**DON'T**
42. Follow through with personal commitments <u>or</u> come back, explain, take the pain and learn from it	42. Blame someone else
43. Ask people, "take me… show me"	43. Make assumptions
44. Ask open-ended questions	44. Refrain from asking questions because you think it undermines your position
45. Be honest with yourself; know what you do know and what you don't	45. Be defensive
46. Learn from others and develop tricks that work for you	46. Think there is just one way to succeed
47. Tell people up front your need to understand - task, job, process and procedures	47. Try to cover up what you don't know
48. Be open - listen to feedback from people	48. Dismiss people's feedback and ideas
49. Contain problems and identify permanent fixes	49. "Band-aid" problems – provide only "get-by" solutions
50. Create best practices that are standardized, documented and implemented	50. Lose learning by not documenting and sharing issues and solutions

How do I build trust and credibility?

*Lose your wealth and
you've lost nothing.
Lose your health and
you've lost something.
Lose your character and
you've lost everything.*
Ben Lapadula
General Manager of Honey Bucket Farms, California

How do I build trust and credibility?

Leaders who DO everyday leadership know trust and credibility come from doing the right things: Where attitudes and actions match personal *and* organizational values and commitments.

How do I build trust and credibility?

DO	DON'T
1. Be consistently 100% honest	1. Use half-truths, spin or avoid
2. Say "I don't know; I'll find out"	2. Pretend to be someone you're not
3. Lead by example – hold yourself to a higher standard	3. Say one thing and do another
4. Do what's right – stick to decisions or admit mistakes	4. Cut deals with people or be a pushover
5. Commit to the extent of your knowledge and authority	5. Overcommit to things outside your control
6. Make decisions when you need to	6. Freeze and get overrun
7. Circle back to interested parties – with follow-up, feedback, information or an answer	7. Leave people wondering
8. Maintain confidences and trust of those who are absent	8. Break confidences or talk behind people's backs

How do I build trust and credibility?

DO 1:
Be consistently 100% honest

Why? Mark Twain said: "If you tell the truth, you don't have to remember anything." And you won't leave people wondering: "Was that the truth...or not?"

What is "100% honest?" *Always* telling the truth and being clear about what you haven't shared.

What's the DO attitude? Realize that lying may be your attempt to control the situation and dictate what people think and do. Remember that "little white lies" and spinning the truth for your own benefit don't work. With selective honesty, you'll eventually get caught in a lie.

Why is this hard to DO? Sometimes the truth is difficult to say and for others to hear; you may have to point out a flaw in yourself or in others.

What's the DO reward? Daily you create trust with other people. One hundred percent honesty builds strong relationships of trust.

CAUTION! While you should always tell the truth, some information might be shared on a "need to know basis." You don't always have to tell everything you know. Be willing, however, to tell people why you can't tell them something. (For example, you may have privileged information about a job candidate that you cannot share until the information is public.)

MORE CAUTION! Being 100% honest is not a license to use harsh and insensitive statements (e.g., "He's a real jerk!").

- Ask: Do I exaggerate or lie to make myself look better (more knowledgeable or competent)? Do I exaggerate or lie to make others feel better? Why?

- Take the "audience" test: Can you say what you want to say in a room full of your peers, your boss, your parents or your kids?

- Assume people you talk to *will* compare notes. What will they think if and when their notes don't match? (e.g., You told Todd there wasn't a budget crisis. You told Cassandra we needed to slash overhead by 40%.)

- Keep track of your discussions, commitments and lessons learned. Review them weekly for honest and consistent decision-making. Ask yourself:

  * Am I truthful?
  * Do I deal openly and fairly with others?
  * Do I value and reward people for their honesty?

- Your success:

Connected DOs:
9—Trust people and check their work when necessary
40—Be completely clear about your follow-up—what you will do and won't do
45—Be honest with yourself; know what you do know and what you don't

DON'T 1:
Use half truths, spin or avoid

How do I build trust and credibility?

DO 2:
Say "I don't know; I'll find out"

Why? If you fake that you know, eventually you will get caught, and team members won't believe you even when you're right.

What's the DO attitude? "Fake it until you make it" doesn't work for this DO. If you don't know something, admit it. Then go find the answer and follow up with whomever needs to know.

Why is this hard to DO? Your pride can make it difficult to admit that you don't know something. It takes more time initially to track down answers than to pretend you know something.

What's the DO reward? People will trust what you DO say. You will get the information needed to make the right decisions. Plus, people hate it when you pretend to know something you don't.

CAUTION! Don't use "I don't know" as a cop-out for dealing with difficult issues.

- Work out why you have a hard time saying "I don't know." Is the pressure to know everything internal (e.g., ego, insecurity) or external (e.g., prestige, power, peers)? When you know what drives your actions, you'll know what to change.

- Ask your boss: What should I know in my position and what are your expectations?

- Ask your team: As your boss what are your expectations of me?

- Adopt the *Answer Golden Rule*: "Give answers to others as you would have them give answers to you."

- Keep track of questions you committed to answering and the date/time when you answered them.

- Your success:

_____

_____

Connected DOs:
19—Ask for help
30—Face up to issues and deal with them
44—Ask open-ended questions

DON'T 2:
Pretend to be someone
you are not

How do I build trust and credibility?

DO 3:
Lead by example—
hold yourself to a higher standard

Why? Your actions and your work carry more weight than your words.

What is "a higher standard?" A "no excuses" attitude— exceeding expectations even when it's tough, when others fall short or when the consequences seem small. Strive for the maximum return on investment instead of the minimum.

What's the DO attitude? People look to leaders to model standards for performance. You must set the example by which you want others to work and live.

Why is this hard to DO? A higher standard may seem like extra work: Why do more when others are doing less?

What's the DO reward? You'll have personal pride and satisfaction from a job well done, as well as a clear conscience when you look people in the eye and challenge them to do their best.

CAUTION! Evaluate what standards you really want to set for your team. Be careful your standards don't create unnecessary detail, more worry or more work.

- Lead in ways you wouldn't be ashamed for others to see— remind yourself that "you *always* have a choice."

- Adopt the **Stop**, **Think** and **Choose** tool:
  Stop—create a choice space; e.g., count to ten
  Think—remember the DOs; ensure you understand the situation
  Choose—follow through and use the DO

- Work alongside your people on a regular basis (e.g., When there's a client mailing to collate, take a break from your work and lend a hand).

- Be the *first* to volunteer, ask questions and engage others.

- Don't ask others to do things you wouldn't do yourself (e.g., consistently require your team members to work late while you go home on time).

- Teach always—if necessary, use words (paraphrase of St. Francis of Assisi).

- Your success:

_____

_____

Connected DOs:
20—Choose your own behavior, demonstrate a positive attitude and work to influence others
32—Put the organization and its people first
50—Create best practices that are standardized, documented and implemented

DON'T 3:
Say one thing and do another

How do I build trust and credibility?

DO 4:
Do what's right—
stick to decisions or admit mistakes

Why? You may not recover from cutting deals; value-based decisions give you long-term respect as a trusted leader.

What does "cut deals" mean? Making exceptions to the organization's rules. For example, "I'll let you leave fifteen minutes early if you meet your quality quota for the shift."

What's the DO attitude? Compromise is essential when working with people and getting work done. However, you must understand what is not worth compromising both personally and professionally. You must not let working toward compromise paralyze you with indecision—you'll muddy the waters, create uncertainty and lower productivity. Instead, tell your employees your expectations so they can focus their work.

Why is this hard to DO? It may seem easier to avoid conflict and make people happy in the short run rather than stick with what you know is right in the long run. Or if you do what's right, you may be standing alone if others walk away.

What's the DO reward? Your conscience will be clear and you'll be satisfied with standing up for what you know is right.

CAUTION! Pick your battles—not every issue is a mountain!

MORE CAUTION! "Do what's right" is not the same as "What I say is right" or "What I say goes." You have to be willing to listen and learn.

- Ask: Would you make the same decision if you knew it would be the lead story in tomorrow's newspaper or the company newsletter?

- Review your goals when making decisions. Ask: "How will this impact our short- and long-term success? How will this affect my credibility? How does what I do now impact other events later?"

- What are the long-term consequences of "cutting deals?" If you make a deal, make sure you understand the positive and negative outcomes and who it will affect.

- Strike a balance: If you think it is the right decision, stick to it *and* still be willing to listen to others, understand their points of view and be influenced.

- Remember: A pattern of cutting deals or giving in is often unfair to your people; it rewards negative behaviors and punishes those who try to do the right thing.

- Your success:

_____

_____

Connected DOs:
20—Choose your own behavior, demonstrate a positive attitude and work to influence others
21—Focus your efforts—pick your issues and your time
26—Insist on accountability and potential solutions for problems, then help with the right things

DON'T 4:
Cut deals with people
or be a pushover

How do I build trust and credibility?

DO 5:
Commit to the extent of your knowledge and authority

Why? You will build relationships of trust—both as a credible leader and one who can be counted on to follow through.

What does "extent of your knowledge and authority" mean? Knowing what you know, what you don't, and what power and influence you have to make decisions.

What's the DO attitude? You cannot be, do or decide everything. When you step up to the responsibilities of your role, you make and deliver on commitments. You have a clear idea of what you cannot commit to because it lies outside your realm of responsibility and authority.

Why is this hard to DO? You need to accept your personal limits for knowledge and authority.

What's the DO reward? You will be respected for genuinely using your strengths and asking others to use theirs.

CAUTION! Don't forget to stretch yourself—while you may not have the knowledge, you can always learn something new!

- Asking for help is a *strength*, not a weakness; you don't have to know it all, just when and where to find the information you need.

- When you do step up, accept the accountability and the consequences.

- List your skills and knowledge and then rate each using a scale such as excellent, good, fair and poor; use this list as a guide when making commitments; post a personal action plan to improve areas that are not your strengths (see FACET™ tool, page 63); an example follows.

  My Know-How:
  Injection molding, line #3—excellent
  Union rules—good
  Quality standards, line #7—fair

  My Improvement Plan:
  Read quality manual for line #7 on Monday
  Job shadow Redmond on line #7 on Tuesday

- Manage up or across the leadership ladder when a decision is not within your authority (e.g., an employee asks you about overtime hours each week; tell her that Gloria Smith in Human Resources can answer her question).

- Your success:

_____

_____

Connected DOs:
19—Ask for help
32—Put the organization and its people first
45—Be honest with yourself; know what you do know and what you don't

DON'T 5:
Overcommit to things outside your control

How do I build trust and credibility?

DO 6:
Make decisions when you need to

Why? Timely decisions move the organization forward and keep you out of analysis paralysis.

What's the DO attitude? First, be decisive at the right time. A right decision at the wrong time is often the wrong decision. Some issues gain momentum over time so they need be tackled early (e.g., personal conflict).

Second, recognize you may have to make a decision before you have all the information or when there isn't a consensus.

Third, if your decision has unintended negative consequences, make a new decision, apologize if needed and learn from the experience.

Why is this hard to DO? You can feel anxious about being seen to be wrong. You have to have the courage to fail.

What's the DO reward? You will deal with the right things at the right time.

CAUTION! Don't make all the decisions: Know which ones you should make yourself, which ones you should delegate, and which ones need involvement of people above you in the chain of command.

MORE CAUTION! Recognize the reality and timing of the situation—but don't make poor decisions by unnecessarily making them under pressure.

- When you begin a new project, ask your team key questions like:

  MAGNITUDE: How significant is this decision? What's the impact?

  URGENCY: How critical is this? Is it a fire that needs quick attention? Do we have a day, week or month?

  RESOURCES: What help do we need? (Money, information, people, equipment, time)

- What's the worst thing that could happen? Indecision comes from fear—evaluate what you fear and deal with that first.

- Practice "worst case" scenarios in advance - "What do I do if…" (e.g., I'm short two employees today OR Four clients are overdue on payments, and we can't make payroll this month).

- Gather your thoughts and take a deep breath when you're finding it difficult to make a decision; ask for ten minutes of "thinking time" during a meeting (e.g., leave the room).

- Your success:

_____

_____

Connected DOs:
30—Face up to issues and deal with them
32—Put the organization and its people first
42—Follow through with personal commitments or come back, explain, take the pain and learn from it

DON'T 6:
Freeze and get overrun

How do I build trust and credibility?

DO 7:
Circle back to interested parties—with follow-up, feedback, information or an answer

Why? Quality follow-up builds people's confidence and trust in you.

What's the DO attitude? Uncertainty makes people nervous and indecisive—creating a distraction for you and for them. Be a consistent communicator and use follow-up as a tool to close the loop and minimize others' anxiety.

Why is this hard to DO? It takes time and energy to get back to people.

What's the DO reward? Your people will get answers to their questions and be more productive because they're not left wondering.

CAUTION! Share only the right level of detail. If you share too much detail, you'll waste time and overload the stakeholder. If you don't share enough detail, the stakeholder may not have enough information to be confident in your results.

- List key stakeholders and what they need to know about the status of your projects.

- Use the ICUC™ tool to be certain you and your stakeholders see the same picture and understand the same things (see page 39).

- Write your communication commitments down; create a checklist or action register in your planner and build next steps into meeting agendas and daily priorities.

- Schedule a specific date for your follow-up; review your follow-up due dates as part of your daily game plan.

- Call early to set up an alternative timeline if you won't find an answer by the deadline.

- Your success:

_____

_____

Connected DOs:
19—Ask for help
29—Prepare and start the day with a game plan—to dos
36—Work through issues <u>with</u> people; listen first, then discuss

DON'T 7:
Leave people wondering

ICUC™

The goal of ICUC™ is to get on the same page—"what I see, you see." ICUC™ is: Individualized, Context, Unmistakable and Close the Loop. Here are some tips to use ICUC™:

Individualized

- Get into the other's perspective. Ask yourself:
  * How will this sound to him?
  * What does he need to hear to understand this?
  * How could he best hear this?
- Use examples from the other person's world—something familiar.
- As a listener adapt your listening style to the speaker.

Context

- Share the rest of the story—the background that sets the stage.
- Explain why this is happening or why it's important.
- Use plain language or define concepts, terms or jargon.
- As a listener ask for the context and background information.

Unmistakable

- Add details and specificity that provide clarity.
- Be SMART (Specific, Measurable, Actionable, Results-Based and Time Bound).
- Explain words that could have more than one meaning.
- Provide a specific example to illustrate your message.
- When listening, ask questions if it's confusing or vague.

Close the Loop (see also page 133)

- When summarizing understanding, Individualize your delivery, include Context and make the message Unmistakable.
- Look for Close the Loop feedback: Responses like "that's it" or "exactly" mean you summarized the message well.

I'm not upset that you lied to me.
I'm upset that from now on
I can't believe you.
Friedrich Nietzsche
Prussian philologist and philosopher

How do I build trust and credibility?

DO 8:
Maintain confidences and trust of those who are absent

Why? You'll be respected for your integrity with relationships of trust.

What's the DO attitude? People's confidence and trust are fragile and priceless. When others trust you, they will share with you what's really happening. And they will listen to you and be influenced by what you have to say.

Even with the best intentions, however, it can be tempting to break confidences or talk behind people's backs. While it may seem helpful to get certain information to people, it is a poor trade-off. Your indiscretion will mean you can't be *completely* trusted.

What happens when you do the DON'T? If you tell one person privileged information - a secret - that one person will likely tell a trusted friend, who will tell her trusted friend, and so on. Before you know it, several people will know the proprietary information.

Why is this hard to DO? When someone is absent, it's easy to forget about her opinions and feelings. It can feel like stress relief to share information about someone to another person who will listen.

What's the DO reward? You enhance your credibility and build trust and confidence with your co-workers. You also set the example of how you want to be treated.

CAUTION! You have a duty of care to ensure people are not being abused or injured and that ethical violations are reported.

- Take the "mirror test." Can you look in the mirror and say to yourself exactly what you'd say to others?

- Write a checklist of the team members who are absent from the meeting; send them a copy of the minutes and next steps.

- Tell people to speak directly to the person with whom they have an issue; if it cannot be resolved one-on-one, agree upon a neutral party to listen; if they still cannot resolve the issue, speak to your boss or hire a third party facilitator.

- Instead of breaking a confidence, ask for permission to share sensitive information.

- Your success:

Connected DOs:
9—Trust people and check their work when necessary
14—Treat people with respect and tell them when they've done a good job
20—Choose your own behavior, demonstrate a positive attitude and work to influence others

DON'T 8:
Break confidences or
talk behind people's backs

We have too many high sounding words and too few actions that correspond with them.

Abigail Adams

Former U.S. First Lady

How do I get my people working together as a team?

Teamwork is the ability to work together toward a common vision. It is the fuel that allows common people to attain uncommon results.
Andrew Carnegie
Businessperson and philanthropist

How do I get my people working together as a team?

Leaders who DO everyday leadership get the most from their people and know their own strengths and weaknesses, as well as those of their team.

How do I get my people working together as a team?

DO	DON'T
9. Trust people and check their work when necessary	9. Let people chase you away
10. Learn people's first names and greet everyone, every day, as a priority	10. Wait until making assignments to interact with people
11. Know who your people are, their qualifications, jobs and where they're located	11. Be unaware of who your people are
12. Get to know your people on a personal level	12. Be buddies or a stranger
13. Spend time side-by-side with people	13. Spend all your time in your office
14. Treat people with respect and tell them when they've done a good job	14. Treat people like they're idiots
15. Give out work assignments, document accountability and hold people accountable	15. Duck responsibility for ensuring work gets done and hope it works out
16. Solicit ideas from others to shape decisions	16. Shut people down
17. Set expectations and boundaries for jobs and provide necessary information	17. Tell people "just do it" or how to do it

How do I get my people working together as a team?

DO 9:
Trust people and check their work
when necessary

Why? You will build strong relationships, maximize people's abilities, learn more and ensure the work gets done.

What does "check their work" mean? Use hard data or direct observation to evaluate work against expectations.

What's the DO attitude? You cannot take a "hands-off" approach when it comes to your people's work. You are responsible for the performance and progress of your people.

Why is this hard to DO? Some employees will be uncomfortable when you watch their work or evaluate them. This can create friction and strain your relationship instead of building a connection.

What's the DO reward? You will understand what work is being done and how it's being accomplished, while investing time to build relationships and employees' skills.

CAUTION! Be concerned if people always wait for you to leave before they start their work!

- Don't spend all day in your office—set aside time each day or a block of time each week to talk with people and discuss what they do.

- Ask questions to connect with team members, learn about their skills and evaluate the quality of their work:
  "I'm interested in how you do this…"
  "I'll stay for ten minutes to make sure what I said was clear…"

- Use your time wisely; be selective of what you observe—review key areas to give you an accurate assessment of what's happening (e.g., "Show me your first draft" or "Show me the equipment that slows you down").

- Your success:

Connected DOs:
25—Collect the information needed for any given task from your people
27—Be consistent with expectations, but adjust approach to the individual
43—Ask people, "take me…show me"

DON'T 9:
Let people chase you away

How do I get my people working together as a team?

DO 10:
Learn people's first names and greet everyone, every day, as a priority

Why? When you use a person's name, you make a connection and show that you value and respect them.

What's the DO attitude? Make people your first priority. Recognize that your team members don't want to be treated as a number, a worker or a cog in a machine. Using people's names creates an instant positive reaction—a look up, a head turn and a smile.

Why is this hard to DO? It's easy to focus on work and forget about the importance of touching base with your people. If you don't make a concerted effort, people's names are easy to forget.

What's the DO reward? Team members who are valued and respected are generally more productive and loyal.

- Think about how impressed you've been when someone remembered your name and a detail or two about you.

- Ask: Have you ever missed an opportunity because you didn't know someone's name and then avoided him? (e.g., You went to a networking party and couldn't remember Philippe's name, so you steered clear of him all evening.)

- Change where you park to force you to walk through a different area of the work site.

- Schedule time in the first part of your day to walk around and check in with people; visit a different area each morning.

- Use people's first names when you meet them; say a person's name a number of times in your first interaction.

- Know your people; keep notes of your employees' names, strengths, interests and educational backgrounds.

- Use the "Name Game" for a new project team (see page 51).

- Your success:

_____

_____

Connected DOs:
32—Put the organization and its people first
35—Work with key stakeholders and other resources (e.g., departments, people)
43—Ask people, "take me...show me"

DON'T 10:
Wait until making assignments
to interact with people

Name Game

A new team has formed—some team members know each other and some do not. Use the *Name Game* to rapidly learn each teammate's name and something about him or her.

- Pick one person to begin.
- Go around the table.
- First person: Introduce self, including name, department or position, and something unique that most people don't know.
- Second person: Introduce self, using same information as above, then summarize the first person's information.
- Third person: Introduce self, using same information as above, then summarize first and second person's information.
- Continue until all group members have been introduced.

Example

Susan: "I'm Susan McCracken. I work in Research and Development. I was once a NYC taxi cab driver for a summer job."

Tim: "I'm Tim Bakowski. I work in Marketing. I'm a black belt in Karate. This is Susan McCracken. She works in R&D and once drove a taxi for the summer."

Bill: "I'm Bill Sommers. I work in Finance. I'm a NASCAR race fan and have visited all the major race tracks. This is Tim Bakowski from Marketing. He's a black belt. And this is Susan McCracken from R&D. She's a former cab driver."

Shonda: "I'm Shonda Jackson. I work in Logistics. I raise AMC collies. This is Bill Sommers in Finance who is a NASCAR fan. And Tim Bakowski in Marketing, who's a black belt. This is Susan McCracken in R&D who used to drive a taxi."

*A lot of people have gone further
than they thought they could because
someone else thought they could.*

Zig Ziglar

Author and sales consultant

How do I get my people working together as a team?

DO 11:
Know who your people are, their qualifications, job and where they are located

Why? When you know your resources, you can maximize their use.

What does "know who your people are" mean? Be familiar with who works for you and their individual job skills, talents and office or job locations. Know their "hot" buttons—their passions and their needs.

What's the DO attitude? Know your people, get your results. Listen. If you hear: "My boss doesn't know who I am or what I do," your team member is really saying he doesn't feel valued and that you are not a trusted leader.

Why is this hard to DO? Time and energy. Also, people change jobs frequently and learn new skills, and many people may report to you.

What's the DO reward? You will be able to connect with their WIIFM (What's In It For Me?). Your interest will impress your people and cement their loyalty.

CAUTION! Remember the "80/20" rule: Focus on 20% of the work that gives you 80% of the results. If you have more people than you can reasonably know, rely on the informal leaders in your group to keep you informed.

- Meet your team member at her work station to ask a question or respond to a question she's asked.

- Keep an "address book," spreadsheet or record in your PDA to capture details about each employee: list individual job description, location (e.g., plant, line number), skills, unique attributes (e.g., pets, children, hobbies, volunteer activities), training and goals; use this information to stay connected and to support promotions and job transfers.

- Periodically schedule a visit to each worksite to observe or work side-by-side with team members. Ask: Who could step up to fill a gap? What do my people need to prepare them for future opportunities?

- Your success:

_____

_____

Connected DOs:
27—Be consistent with expectations, but adjust approach to the individual
34—Get the right people involved and on the same page
43—Ask people, "take me...show me"

DON'T 11:
Be unaware of who your people are

How do I get my people working together as a team?

DO 12:
Get to know your people
on a personal level

Why? Your job will be easier when you treat people as individuals, understand what motivates them and know when to offer help.

What's the DO attitude? To "know your people on a personal level" means: "I value you. You are important."

Why is this hard to DO? Time and other priorities. People have a sweet spot for familiarity that varies from person to person—too much familiarity is uncomfortable and too little is cold. It can be difficult to find a balance between too many personal connections with some and not enough with others.

What's the DO reward? When you build connections, you establish long-term loyalty, accountability, and balanced lives.

CAUTION! Don't play favorites or you'll sabotage the effectiveness of your team; those who know you on a more personal level might think you owe them special treatment (e.g., bending the organization's rules).

MORE CAUTION! If people do become your friends, it's up to you to clearly and visibly demonstrate that you have a responsibility for the business that goes beyond the scope of friendship.

STILL MORE CAUTION! It's a two-way street; people also need to know you on a personal level so they can build a relationship of trust.

- Regularly take a coffee break or have lunch with your direct reports and ask questions about their interests outside of work.

- Know the significant people and events in the lives of your team. For example, ask "What's on your radar?" at staff meetings and let each person share a one-minute update of work-related projects and one-minute update of non-work projects (e.g., Joe: "We are meeting our targets for the school construction budget…My horse placed first in the state show last Saturday…").

- Schedule annual social events (e.g., family potluck, water park outing, baseball game) with team members and their significant others.

- Celebrate team members' milestones like birthdays, weddings, graduations, purchase of a new home and births.

- If you are a peer who then becomes a boss, remember to tread carefully; make work-related decisions with your head and friendship decisions with your heart.

- Your success:

Connected DOs:
27—Be consistent with expectations, but adjust approach to the individual
32—Put the organization and its people first
34—Get the right people involved and on the same page

DON'T 12:
Be buddies or strangers

How do I get my people working together as a team?

DO 13:
Spend time side-by-side with people

Why? You will build respect and credibility, have a real sense of the issues and know how best to use everyone's abilities.

What's the DO attitude? Your overall success is connected to the work of others: your people's eyes, ears, hands, skills, thinking and experience. To be effective, then, you need to ask: (1) How connected am I with my people? (2) How well do I understand my environment?

Why is this hard to DO? You already have a lot of work to do.

What's the DO reward? You will build strong connections with your team members. Because you know what they are doing, you can direct their work for better results.

CAUTION! Don't look over someone's shoulder and annoy or distract him. Instead, work at a task or project *with* him.

- Set up a regular "job shadow" to understand the specific skills and needs of each of your team members' jobs; tell your team what you learned from job shadowing.

- Meet a team member at her work station or office when you have information to share with her.

- Have an "open door" policy—be available to talk to all employees one-on-one.

- Be a great listener and ask people to *show* you a problem, issue or insight—people will *tell* you everything you need to know.

- Develop a list of insightful, open-ended questions to understand what's really happening; examples include:

    * "If you owned the company, what two or three changes would you make immediately?"
    * "What work issue keeps you awake at night?"

- Keep a notebook handy to capture important information and document actions—yours and others.

- If you are responsible for multiple sites, visit each location and talk with *all* people (not just the leadership); schedule periodic meetings and work sessions at these locations.

- Your success:

Connected DOs:
27—Be consistent with expectations, but adjust approach to the individual
43—Ask people, "take me...show me"
44—Ask open-ended questions
47—Tell people up front your need to understand - task, job, process and procedures

DON'T 13:
Spend all your time in your office

How do I get my people working together as a team?

DO 14:
Treat people with respect—
and tell them when they've done a good job

Why? Respect creates loyalty and motivation to do more good work.

What's the DO attitude? How you treat people usually determines what they'll give you in return. Show respect by following the *Golden Rule*: Treat people as you would like to be treated—listen, explain and trust.

Why is this hard to DO? You may assume it's your job to notice negative behaviors and correct people. Or you may think: "These people don't get it. They don't care," and your words and actions will reflect that view.

What's the DO reward? You'll get respect and people will give 110%.

CAUTION! Respect doesn't equal blind trust: Trust *and* verify.

MORE CAUTION! Despite showing them respect, some people may continue to act like idiots.

STILL MORE CAUTION! Don't give "good job" kudos thoughtlessly. When you compliment someone, really mean it!

- When frustrated, ask: Are my emotions directed toward the people or the problem? How can I focus on the problem and not just the people?

- When a team member does make a mistake, calmly talk with him one-on-one; remember that everyone makes mistakes.

- Instead of only giving out instructions, also give responsibility for a specific result (e.g., Show me an error-free, detailed report with your recommendations by 2:30 p.m. tomorrow.).

- Assign someone who naturally recognizes success in others to record successes and share them with you—let him help you "catch" people doing the right things.

- Share a compliment without attaching criticism; discuss the criticism later or the compliment will be lost.

- Tell the person face-to-face when she's done a good job and be specific (e.g., "Great job creating the list of ten cost-saving ideas! I'm looking forward to implementing them with you.").

- Post or share publicly what team members have taught you (e.g., "Suri showed me the quality standards for Line #3 and explained why we no longer do checks every ten minutes.").

- Honor a "Team Member of the Week" with a traveling trophy.

- Ask your team to tell people when they appreciate their efforts (e.g., Faith says: "Thanks to Al for typing our meeting notes.").

- Your success:

Connected DOs:
22—Defuse situations and deal with people one-on-one
23—Focus on the issue and not the person: "I'm not mad at you, but this behavior is unacceptable because…"
38—Listen and understand first, then act

DON'T 14:
Treat people like they're idiots

How do I get my people working together as a team?

DO 15:
Give out work assignments, document accountability and hold people accountable

Why? Your employees will understand the expectations you have for their performance. And there will be no surprises when you hold them accountable for their results.

What's the DO attitude? Most people have good intentions for their work, but need clarity and requirements for accountability to do their best. Your detailed assignments, accountabilities and follow-up will help them do great work and feel rewarded.

For the minority who would rather avoid work and accountability altogether, creating clear expectations with documentation and follow-up is essential to hold them accountable.

Why is this hard to DO? You must invest the time to be specific in job expectations, performance metrics and follow-up. Sometimes you have to confront people when they don't do their jobs, which is uncomfortable for most people.

What's the DO reward? You will have solid metrics for performance reviews, as well as a focused team.

CAUTION! Define expectations AND leave opportunities for creativity, innovation and personalization so people can uniquely achieve job responsibilities and personal goals.

- Record 3 to 5 key expectations for each job and how they relate to the team's goals; write these on a 3"x5" card or something similar and give them to team members to hang at their work stations; an example follows.

  Parts Assembler
  On time—share shift information
  No errors—reduce costs
  8,000 units/shift—meet sales goals
  One cost savings idea/quarter—increase profits/bonus

- Schedule a "Pulse Check" with each team member; ask employees to be prepared with a work update, feedback and questions.

- Plan quarterly work sessions to review team members' performance and assign steps for improvement.

- When an accountability issue arises, use the FACET™ tool to change negative thinking or behavior (see worksheet on page 63 or download at www.humanergy.com).

- Your success:

Connected DOs:
21—Focus your efforts—pick your issues and your time
26—Insist on accountability and potential solutions for problems, then help with the right things
35—Work with key stakeholders and other resources (e.g., departments, people)

DON'T 15:
Duck responsibility for ensuring work gets done and hope it works out

FACET™ Tool

	FACET™	What you will do
F	**FOCUS** *Choose one change in thinking and behavior*	The **DO** I am going to improve in the next three weeks is: DO # _____.
A	**ACCOUNTABILITY** *Tell someone who will remind you to do what you said you will do*	I will ask _____ to check me on my progress.
C	**CONSEQUENCES** *Choose positive and negative rewards for your actions*	When I **do the DO**, I will reward myself by _____ _____. When I **don't do the DO**, I will penalize myself by _____ _____.
E	**EASIER TO DO** *Eliminate the roadblocks to your success*	I will stop or eliminate _____ _____ to help me **do the DO**.
T	**TRACKING** *Record your progress*	When I **do the DO**, I will track my success by _____ _____.

Leaders must be close enough to relate to others, but far enough ahead to motivate them.

John C. Maxwell
Pastor, trainer and founder of INJOY

How do I get my people working together as a team?

DO 16:
Solicit ideas from others
to shape decisions

Why? An issue multiplied by different viewpoints equals the best result.

What's the DO attitude? Open your mind; ask for ideas and alternative solutions. Understand that if you shut people down because you don't need or want their input, they might not give you feedback when the situation is critical and their input would be invaluable.

Why is this hard to DO? Time; it's faster to decide everything yourself.

What's the DO reward? Team members will appreciate being asked for their opinions and suggestions. You'll develop the most informed and innovative solutions.

CAUTION! Practice on the simple decisions to prepare the team for more difficult, high-stake and high-pressure situations.

MORE CAUTION! Don't overuse this idea for simple and low-cost decisions. Use your judgment for an issue that is important enough to get multiple ideas.

- Decide if you have the right information to shape decisions:
    * Do you have the right people in the room?
    * Do you value the various perspectives each person brings?
    * Have you done everything to maximize participation?
    * Are you making the best use of multiple views?

- When the right people are in the right room at the right time, then:

  * Unlock thinking with: "What if…" "Let go…" "Imagine…"
  * Eliminate assumptions (e.g., "Poncho is too young to give us any valuable input," or "We've always done it that way.").
  * Remove distractions (e.g., cell phones, laptops, PDAs).
  * Add creative thinking (e.g., brainstorm, small groups of three to five).

- Ask each team member to come to a meeting prepared with two possible solutions to an impending problem (e.g., "We're losing funding for the music program in six months. What can we do?").

- Engage your team members by asking open-ended questions (see DO 44).

- Practice BrainBuilding™ in team meetings (see page 125).

- Your success:

Connected DOs:
2—Say "I don't know; I'll find out"
19—Ask for help
35—Work with key stakeholders and other resources (e.g., departments, people)
44—Ask open-ended questions

DON'T 16:
Shut people down

How do I get my people working together as a team?

DO 17:
Set expectations and boundaries for jobs and provide necessary information

Why? Your employees will do great work and work toward their potential.

What are "expectations and boundaries?" Results you want an employee to achieve and the framework he can use to achieve them.

What's the DO attitude? Give others just enough guidance to be successful and then get out of the way.

Why is this hard to DO? It's challenging to find time to discuss each job with each employee and guide her based on her unique skills, talents, experience and goals.

What's the DO reward? Employees will be clear about their roles in the organization and the results they need to achieve.

CAUTION! Too many boundaries stifle creativity and innovation. Don't get caught in the details and miss opportunities for improved efficiencies or new product and service ideas.

MORE CAUTION! Too few boundaries will increase frustration and make employees feel as if they have to "sink or swim."

- Organize a job packet for each specific job—include company information, key accountabilities and growth opportunities; give the packet to employees who are new to a job.

- Make it a habit to share a detailed picture of what's needed and why it's important; ask employees "What do you think we need in order to deliver?".

- Use the **DESIRED™** coaching tool (**D**escribe, **E**xplain, **S**how, **I**mitate, **R**ectify, **E**valuate and **D**elegate) to show performance expectations and watch how they do it (see page 69 or www.humanergy.com for a DESIRED™ worksheet).

- Summarize performance feedback and compare against expectations: What's going well? What can be improved?

- Write **SMART** goals for clarity and understanding:

  S— Specific (precise, short, clear description)

  M— Measurable (numerical, observable, business-focused)

  A— Achievable (within influence, raises performance)

  R— Results-based (the future state, what you want to achieve)

  T— Time-bound (dates and times)

- Your success:

Connected DOs:
25—Collect the information needed for any given task from your people
26—Insist on accountability and potential solutions for problems, then help with the right things
47—Tell people up front your need to understand—e.g., task, job, process and procedures

DON'T 17:
Tell people "just do it" or how to do it

DESIRED™ Coaching Tool

DESIRED™ is a step-by-step communication method to achieve the results you want. In seven steps, **Describe**, **Explain**, **Show**, **Imitate**, **Rectify**, **Evaluate** and **Delegate**, you can successfully coach a team member, begin a new project, complete an effective performance review and introduce a new employee.

Describe what results the 'performer' needs to achieve. Give clear standards for success.

Explain why the results are important and the positive and negative outcomes for performance.

Show her the best way to get the results.

Imitate Ask her to perform what you have shown her.

Rectify performance, reinforcing good work and correcting mistakes.

Evaluate performance, testing it against standards.

Delegate the work when she is competent, holding her accountable for success!

Never tell people how to do things. Tell them what to do, and they'll surprise you with their ingenuity.
George S. Patton
Former U.S. General

*A coach is someone who can give
correction without causing resentment.*
John Wooden
Author and former UCLA basketball coach

How do I keep perspective on what's important?

The pessimist sees difficulty in every opportunity. The optimist sees the opportunity in every difficulty.
Winston Churchill
Former Prime Minister of Great Britain and author

How do I keep perspective on what's important?

Leaders who DO everyday leadership use judgment to make quality and consistent decisions that are reality-based, insightful, and balance the risks and the benefits.

How do I keep perspective on what's important?

DO	DON'T
18. Stay open-minded when receiving feedback	18. Make or take it personally
19. Ask for help	19. Try and do it by yourself
20. Choose your own behavior, demonstrate a positive attitude and work to influence others	20. React to other people and let them push your buttons
21. Focus your efforts – pick your issues and your time	21. React to everything and lose your focus
22. Defuse situations and deal with people one-on-one	22. Let disruptive people have an audience
23. Focus on the issue and not the person: "I'm not mad at you, but this behavior is unacceptable because…"	23. Make conflict personal and emotional

How do I keep perspective on what's important?

DO 18:
Stay open-minded when receiving feedback

Why? If you allow yourself to get caught in the emotions of an issue, your judgment will be clouded. You'll ignore facts that don't match your feelings, and it will be difficult to see possible solutions.

What's the DO attitude? When you care, you take ownership and invest in your work. A natural response, then, is to take things personally when something goes wrong. Taking it personally can undermine your ability to do your best because your emotional reaction is in the driver's seat, while what's important is in the back.

Why is this hard to DO? When you are challenged, defensive reactions can be triggered. You might feel like you are being attacked, and your judgment or ability is being questioned.

What's the DO reward? You'll be in control of your emotions and tackle the issues with a clear mind.

CAUTION! Don't ignore your emotions! Instead, be aware—when you find yourself taking an issue personally, put the emotional reaction "on hold" and deal with the facts.

- Ask a neutral person to be your sounding board; share your concerns and let that person remind you of what's *really* critical, then sleep on important decisions.

- Be sure issues are handled at the right level of detail and with the right people so you can stay focused on things you *need* to do; otherwise, you will be overwhelmed and more likely to react emotionally when you receive feedback.

- Check these seven questions to adjust your focus:

  * What's important to you personally?
  * What's important to the organization?
  * Why are you doing this?
  * What do you really want to achieve?
  * What do you want it to look like when you're done?
  * Will this issue be important next week, in a month or next year?
  * Does your team understand the priorities?

- Understand your "hot" buttons and take a "time out" when they are pushed; practice responses to refocus yourself (e.g., "I have a hard time dealing with negative feedback, so I will practice saying, 'I will focus on the issue and not the person,' to stay calm.").

- When you feel yourself overreacting emotionally, take a deep breath and focus on listening to the other person; then ask for a few minutes of "thinking time" to get your emotions in check.

- Take time for family and friends, healthy eating, exercise, hobbies and sleep.

- Your success:

Connected DOs:
30—Face up to issues and deal with them
32—Put the organization and its people first
33—Accept "this is our assignment" and work to make it succeed

DON'T 18:
Make or take it personally

How do I keep perspective on what's important?

DO 19:
Ask for help

Why? You can't do it all by yourself.

What's the DO attitude? You may be very talented, but you don't know and can't do everything. Some have different experiences and skills. Others have made mistakes and learned valuable lessons. Ask for their help.

Why is this hard to DO? You may think that you should know or be good at everything...or you may not want to "bother" other people by asking for help.

What's the DO reward? You will get the help you need, team members will appreciate your willingness to admit you don't know everything and everyone's strengths will be used.

CAUTION! Sometimes it's better to dig in and figure out something on your own, rather than asking others for help. If you can do it by yourself, do it. If not, ask.

- List resources for your department, job and projects (e.g., boss, peers, predecessors, professional acquaintances); use and learn from your resources.

- Involve people based upon their strengths, passions and long-term interests (e.g., Jerry is a "numbers-person," has a degree in accounting, worked at four of our plants and wants to work in Human Resources to develop hiring policies).

- Model the example of continuous learning and asking for help; use key phrases like:

    * "I'm sure you have good ideas for…"
    * "I'm trying to improve what I'm doing. How would you do it?"

- Ask people who bring you questions about their ideas for possible solutions (e.g., Sarah tells you the shrink wrapper has more errors on odd-shaped units. Ask her how she would solve the problem: "What do you think?").

- Thank the people who help you and let them know what their help accomplished (e.g., "Your input on the proposal helped us cut costs and be more competitive. We got the contract. Good work!").

- Your success:

Connected DOs:
2—Say "I don't know; I'll find out"
16—Solicit ideas from others to shape decisions
35—Work with key stakeholders and other resources (e.g., departments, people)
43—Ask people, "take me...show me"

DON'T 19:
Try and do it by yourself

How do I keep perspective on what's important?

DO 20:
Choose your own behavior, demonstrate a positive attitude and work to influence others

Why? Your attitude and example are contagious! A balanced and positive attitude will influence your team positively. A negative one will influence them negatively. Which attitude would you like for your boss to choose?

What does "work to influence others" mean? By your example, others learn how to contribute positively to the task and bottom line.

What's the DO attitude? When you react to people, you give them control over you. For some, your reaction magnifies their feelings. For others, this is a sport or strategy to keep you from succeeding. Either way, they are in control—not you. Remind yourself: You control your own attitudes and actions. Don't ever give that control away.

Why is this hard to DO? When your buttons are pushed, like reflexes, you have rapid and powerful emotional responses. However, unlike your hard-wired reflexes, like blinking your eyes, emotional responses are voluntary and can be unlearned.

What's the DO reward? Your health will benefit from a positive outlook. You'll create an optimistic work environment focused on opportunities instead of problems.

CAUTION! To balance the day-to-day issues with your vision, use the "Stockdale Paradox" as your guide: "Retain faith that you will prevail in the end, regardless of the difficulties. At the same time confront the most brutal facts of your reality, whatever they might be."

- "I always have a choice"—don't be afraid to stop, think and choose your attitude and actions (see page 30).

- Understand the things people do that upset you (e.g., lying, gossip, swearing); list and practice responses that calm you down (e.g., "I'm not going to take this personally…").

- Schedule fifteen minutes of "think time" to start your day— write your answers to these five questions and check them during the day:

    * What is really important today?
    * Who will I meet today?
    * How will I help others succeed?
    * How will I handle fires or crises?
    * What unresolved issues from yesterday should I deal with today?

- Excuse yourself from a situation when you feel your buttons are being pushed.

- Your success:

_____

_____

Connected DOs:
14—Treat people with respect—and tell them when they've done a good job
24—Step into a job with intensity for success—do what you can to make things better
33—Accept "this is our assignment" and work to make it succeed

DON'T 20:
React to other people and let them push your buttons

How do I keep perspective on what's important?

DO 21:
Focus your efforts—
pick your issues and your time

Why? You can't do it all! If you try, you'll do nothing well and be very frustrated.

What does "focus" mean? Spend your time on what's most important.

What's the DO attitude? Recognize that often the choice of how to spend your time is between the *good* and the *best* use of time. This means that you choose to focus efforts on the *most* high-value issues. You have to decide and accept that it's okay to stop doing some things in order to do the critical few well.

Why is this hard to DO? You may thrive on chaos and confusion, or you might be in a cycle of fire-fighting.

What's the DO reward? You will carry out the organization's important priorities and have your own sense of accomplishment; it's also easier the next time.

CAUTION! Don't have tunnel vision—focusing only on long-term issues may let the day-to-day fires burn out of control.

- Make a "*to do*" list; prioritize and do the tasks that only you can do; delegate the rest.

- Make a "*not to do*" list to keep your focus.

- Push issues down to the appropriate level—set the overall direction and outcomes for the team and allow them to work out the specifics.

- List your department or team's top priorities for the week, month or quarter; post in a visible place.

- Break the cycle—stop doing the busy work, start doing the important work.

- Log how you spend your day to identify where you waste or have unfocused time (e.g., "I spent two hours on budget details I could have had my assistant research instead.").

- Be willing to set aside things you *like to do* to work on the more important tasks first.

- Ask the project focus questions:

    * What work is included? What's not?
    * Whose perspective(s) are you using? Not using?
    * What is the timeline?
    * Do you have an agreed-upon success goal?
    * Are your actions driven by the success goal?

- Your success:

Connected DOs:
29—Prepare and start the day with a game plan—to dos
31—Fight for doing the right thing—if you know about it, you are responsible for it
32—Put the organization and its people first
34—Get the right people involved and on the same page

DON'T 21:
React to everything and lose your focus

How do I keep perspective on what's important?

DO 22:
Defuse situations and deal with people one-on-one

Why? An audience will complicate the conflict and amplify emotions.

What's the DO attitude? Stay calm. When a person is defensive and the conversation is emotionally charged, you can calm him by speaking at your normal rate and listening to his words, tone and body language.

Why is this hard to DO? Your natural response is to get caught in the emotion and be defensive.

What's the DO reward? When you recognize others' fears and work through them, you honor them with respect and dignity.

CAUTION! Don't try to be a hero! For your own protection, ask a third party to intervene so you don't get into a "he said, she said" situation or expose yourself to liability (e.g., if the conflict crosses a moral or legal line).

MORE CAUTION! Don't forget to circle back to the audience and help them understand the situation and its resolution.

What are the three parts to this DO?

(1) **PREVENT** by building in best practices that minimize conflict.
(2) **PREPARE** so you are ready when conflict surfaces.
(3) **MANAGE YOURSELF** because you and your reactions are the only parts of the conflict you can really control.

PREVENT

- Be open—listen to feedback from people (DO 48)

- Use meeting best practices to manage conflict up front (page 139)

- Deal with conflict one-on-one whenever possible; having fewer people involved reduces the complexity of emotions, opinions and complications and increases your chance of working out the issue.

PREPARE

- Recognize which situations are likely to spark conflict and practice phrases to minimize the conflict:

  * "You seem to be upset. Let's talk about this privately."
  * "Please come into my office and tell me about the situation."

MANAGE YOURSELF

- Take three deep breaths—on the first breath, remember what's important; on the second breath, remember what you want to accomplish; and on the third breath, think of how you'll accomplish it.

- Your success:

Connected DOs:
30—Face up to issues and deal with them
36—Work through issues <u>with</u> people; listen first, then discuss
38—Listen and understand first, then act

DON'T 22:
Let disruptive people have an audience

How do I keep perspective on what's important?

DO 23:
Focus on the issue and not the person: "I'm <u>not</u> mad at you, but this behavior is unacceptable because..."

Why? You'll drive positive changes in team members' behaviors.

What's the DO attitude? Separate the person from the problem. Focus on the facts, not the fiction. Use clear language to help the person lower his defenses.

Why is this hard to DO? Your natural reaction is to focus on the person instead of the issue.

What's the DO reward? You will resolve the issue and the employee will feel less threatened, creating a greater commitment to you and the organization.

CAUTION! When people are defensive, they stop listening and shut down their minds. Remember to be patient and keep your cool.

What are the two parts to this DO? (1) PREPARE improves your response in stressful situations. **(2) IN THE HEAT OF THE MOMENT** gives you tools to respond instead of simply reacting.

PREPARE

- List things people do that upset you (e.g., lying, swearing, gossip); write down and practice responses that calm you (e.g., "I'm going to look for the good in this person.").

- If you get too emotional, calm yourself by stepping away briefly or talking to a friend or peer.

- List your fears (e.g., losing your job, looking stupid, feeling unneeded); write down and practice responses that calm you (e.g., "I'm not going to take this personally…").

- Know the things that upset your team members (e.g., playing favorites, giving incomplete information, not squashing rumors).

IN THE HEAT OF THE MOMENT

- You <u>always</u> have a choice:
    Stop (create a choice space; e.g., count to ten before acting).
    Think (remember the DOs; ask for a clear understanding).
    Choose (follow through and use the DOs).

- Acknowledge the other person's fears and emotions: "I know you're upset…" OR "This is not about losing your job, but we need to talk about…"; repeat these statements during the conversation to continue to defuse the conflict.

- Make a fast recovery when you goof, misjudge, take it personally or let your emotions overtake you. Apologize genuinely!

- Your success:

Connected DOs:
14—Treat people with respect—and tell them when they've done a good job
32—Put the organization and its people first
38—Listen and understand first, then act

DON'T 23:
Make conflict personal and emotional

You are in charge of your own attitude, whatever others do or circumstances you face.

Marian Wright Edelman
Founder and President of the Children's Defense Fund

How do I make sure people get things done?

No man will make a great leader who wants to do it all himself or get all the credit for doing it.
Andrew Carnegie
Businessperson and philanthropist

How do I make sure people get things done?

Leaders who DO everyday leadership focus on people by balancing the time between the work that needs to get done and developing relationships with the people who will do the work.

How do I make sure people get things done?

DO	DON'T
24. Step into a job with intensity for success – do what you can to make things better	24. Wait for someone else to do something
25. Collect the information needed for any given task from your people	25. Gloss over necessary details
26. Insist on accountability and potential solutions for problems, then help with the right things	26. Do people's jobs for them
27. Be consistent with expectations, but adjust approach to the individual	27. Work from one size fits all or be inconsistent
28. Write down thoughts, facts and issues – make lists, prioritize and check off	28. Operate without taking notes – rely on memory
29. Prepare and start the day with a game plan – to dos	29. Begin each day with no forethought or preparation

How do I make sure people get things done?

DO 24:
Step into a job with intensity for success—do what you can to make things better

Why? When you take the initiative and focus on success, you are more likely to achieve it.

What does "intensity for success" mean? Attitudes and actions that propel you and the organization forward. You do your best to succeed and don't back down when faced with difficulty.

What's the DO attitude? You take the initiative whenever and however you can to be successful—ask questions, seek information, get help, build relationships, contact others and listen; when the situation requires a decision, you do the best you can, make the decision and act on it.

Why is this hard to DO? It is natural to work with what you know and can control. When you can't control something, you may wait for someone else to do something—limiting both your work and that of your direct reports.

What's the DO reward? You empower your people to do their best.

CAUTION! Some team members will be frustrated with a leader who is "too intense" and forgets common courtesies like respect, taking time to really listen to issues and ideas, and that there's life outside of work. Define your "intensity for success" as a balance between work (e.g., achieving sales goals, cutting costs, retaining productive staff) and life's other priorities (e.g., family, volunteering, hobbies).

- Plan goals with your team and post the goals in public; then publicly track your progress to those goals.

- Meet with each team member individually; ask him for feedback to improve a current process (e.g., weekly staff meeting updates, expense reports, production line efficiencies).

- When you identify a problem, also recommend two or three possible solutions; your solutions don't have to be perfect, but this approach keeps you solution-focused.

- Identify your frustrations with others (e.g., "They're not getting back to me" and "They haven't given me the right training") and turn those into an action plan for you (e.g., "I will follow up with Brenda on Thursday" and "I'll check our department budget for the next project management training session").

- Your success:

Connected DOs:
2—Say "I don't know; I'll find out"
35—Work with key stakeholders and other resources (e.g., departments, people)
42—Follow through with personal commitments or come back, explain, take the pain and learn from it

DON'T 24:
Wait for someone else to do something

How do I make sure people get things done?

DO 25:
Collect all information needed
for any given task from your people

Why? You want to do it right the first time. Time spent at the outset will usually save time later.

What's the DO attitude? Slow down and explain what details you need, why and when you need them. Then use the details to minimize, as well as take advantage of risk and make the best decisions.

Why is this hard to DO? Typically, there's a drive to action, to get going, to do something and get it done. Necessary details can take time to collect and may create impatience and frustration.

What's the DO reward? You will have the information you need to make the best decisions.

CAUTION! Let people know what details are important and valuable. Don't let them waste time by giving you unnecessary information.

- Set up worksheets to collect routine information; use tables and checklists to organize the details.

- Ask questions—talk to peers and others who have done this task before and learn from them.

- When you plan a project and timeline, make sure you have the necessary time built in for fact finding.

- Help people understand the big picture—the "why" behind the need for information; this will help them sort out the necessary details from "the more data, the better."

- Research the Internet to find background or support information from similar projects or issues; join a chat group that discusses your area of interest, project need and expertise.

- Thank people for their input—they're taking time to help you and will be more likely to help you again if their efforts are recognized.

- Your success:

_____

_____

Connected DOs:
34—Get the right people involved and on the same page
35—Work with key stakeholders and other resources (e.g., departments, people)
44—Ask open-ended questions
48—Be open—listen to feedback from people

DON'T 25:
Gloss over necessary details

How do I make sure people get things done?

DO 26:
Insist on accountability and potential solutions for problems, then help with the right things

Why? Your people will achieve the expectations you've set for them.

What are the "right things?" Actions and attitudes that support the ethical and organizational priorities.

What's the DO attitude? Most team members will fulfill the expectations you've set. Expect more and you will get more. Give them the right kind and amount of help so they experience the pride of ownership and the thrill of success.

Why is this hard to DO? It takes time to follow up with people and check on their progress. Asking for updates can put some team members on the defensive: "Doesn't my boss trust me?"

What's the DO reward? The work will get done.

CAUTION! Some people will resist accountability and run from it, especially if former leaders did not hold them accountable.

MORE CAUTION! Remember to lay out the specific expectations, not the specific "how to" get the work done.

STILL MORE CAUTION! Helping with the *right things* does not include doing other people's work for them. Don't fall into the "I'll do it myself because it's easier" trap.

- Identify positive and negative consequences for meeting or not meeting job expectations. Share these with your team.

- Connect with an employee's WIIFM? (What's In It For Me?) to understand her motivations.

- Support employee growth with training and job shadowing.

- Coach others—pass along tips to successfully resolve issues.

- Let employees know you are "here to help," as well as your expectations. When a problem arises, employees should research the issue and provide you with at least two possible solutions.

- When an employee presents you with a problem, take the "monkey test" by asking yourself: "Who is left with the monkey? Who is sweating the issue now?". If the answers are you instead of the employee, then you need to re-evaluate how you help with the right things.

- Use the FACET™ tool (see page 63) to change negative thinking and behavior.

- Your success:

Connected DOs:
13—Spend time side-by-side with people
15—Give out work assignments, document accountability and hold people accountable
50—Create best practices that are standardized, documented and implemented

DON'T 26:
Do people's jobs for them

How do I make sure people get things done?

DO 27:
Be consistent with expectations,
but adjust approach to the individual

Why? Your people want to be treated fairly. Different people require different approaches.

What's the DO attitude? Stretch yourself beyond your leadership comfort zone–the style with which you feel most comfortable. Be able to give people the type of leadership they need.

Why is this hard to DO? You must spend enough time learning about your team members to understand their personalities, skills and abilities as well as how you will adjust your coaching style.

What's the DO reward? Your people will get results in a way that's most comfortable and efficient for them, while maximizing productivity.

CAUTION! Recognize that it's not easy—some may resent you for allowing work to be done in different ways. The method an employee uses may not be the method you prefer.

MORE CAUTION! Watch out for the traps of rewarding your best employees with more work or setting inconsistent performance expectations for the same job.

- Help others understand your intentions and your style by explaining: "This is how I operate…"

- Manage each team member as an individual, rather than a function; tap their unique strengths and allow them flexibility in how the job gets done.

- Write down what you know and need to learn about each team member's background as well as goals to make the best decision for both the individual and the organization.

- Record what people do well and what gets them excited; use this to assign new projects and consider job opportunities.

- Use the ICUC™ tool to communicate (see page 39):
    <u>I</u> — Individualized (tailor, customize)
    <u>C</u> — Context (give background information)
    <u>U</u> — Unmistakable (clear, concise, specific)
    <u>C</u> — Close the Loop (Are you both on the same page?)

- Recognize that people take in, process and share information differently (see DO 34); ask yourself the following questions:

    * Which role is best for this person?
    * What role will stretch this person?
    * What kind of leadership does this person need?
    * How can I best communicate with him?

- Your success:

_____

_____

Connected DOs:
11—Know who your people are, their qualifications, jobs and where they are located
12—Get to know your people on a personal level
13—Spend time side-by-side with people

DON'T 27:
Work from one size fits all or be inconsistent

How do I make sure people get things done?

DO 28:
Write down thoughts, facts and issues—
make lists, prioritize and check off

Why? You will remember information more easily, stay focused on what's important and save time in the long run; your teammates will also trust you to follow through.

What's the DO attitude? Commit to organize: by time, by project, by topic or by people. Decide what best fits your work flow. Be prepared to experiment and change until you find what works for you.

Why is this hard to DO? Writing things down takes time. Most people think they'll remember more than they actually do.

What's the DO reward? You'll increase your IQ! Because important details are written down, you can use your brain power to solve problems and innovate. You will have a record of your work to reference for future promotions.

IMPORTANT NOTE: Success with DO 28 is the foundation for achieving the 49 other DOs!

CAUTION! Unorganized notes will create clutter, confusion and mayhem! Ask yourself two questions:

* How do I make the information easily accessible?
* How do I organize the information so it's quickly searchable?

- Keep a pocket-sized notebook and pen or PDA ready to record notes and summarize key conversations and meetings; this will help you listen, remember, and give you a fact-based reference to track your work.

- Take 15 minutes at the end of each work day to transfer the day's most important points and commitments to a permanent record (e.g., your computer or personal data organizer).

- Use your notes as a reference when considering opportunities to improve your team's productivity, such as employees who deserve a promotion, skills you and your team members need to develop, and who to assign to a new project. Remember that your notes are only useful to the extent they are used.

- Your success:

Connected DOs:
18—Stay open-minded when receiving feedback
21—Focus your efforts—pick your issues and your time
50—Create best practices that are standardized, documented and implemented

DON'T 28:
Operate without taking notes—
rely on memory

How do I make sure people get things done?

DO 29:
Prepare and start the day
with a game plan—to dos

Why? You will know what to do, how to focus your day on what's most important, and when your day has been successful.

What is a "game plan?" A list of prioritized tasks to focus your day.

What's the DO attitude? There are many demands and attention-grabbers at work—plenty to keep you busy. However, being busy doesn't mean you are being productive and doing the important items. A daily game plan helps you focus on what you really need to do and ignore the "noise."

Why is this hard to DO? Planning takes time and effort. A plan means you have to make choices—saying no to some requests and some people.

What's the DO reward? You won't be frustrated by constant "fire-fighting." You'll see your progress as you check off your list.

CAUTION! You still need to put out the "fires." However, when the fire is out, use your plan to bring you back to your priorities.

- Schedule planning time: Review and lay out your priorities for 15 to 30 minutes at the start of your day or at the end of the previous day; if you are too busy once you get to work, find 15 to 30 minutes at home or during the commute to organize and prioritize yourself.

- Use a tool (e.g., Outlook, your PDA or desk calendar) to help you organize your "to dos" and track what gets done.

- Transfer yesterday's still "to dos" onto today's list.

- Schedule time into your mid-day to evaluate the day's objectives and reprioritize as needed.

- If one item has been open for a week or more, decide if you really will or should do it; then schedule time to get it done.

- At the end of the week, schedule one hour to map out your priorities for the week and month ahead.

- Your success:

Connected DOs:
18—Stay open-minded when receiving feedback
21—Focus your efforts—pick your issues and your time
30—Face up to issues and deal with them
42—Follow through with personal commitments or come back, explain, take the pain and learn from it

DON'T 29:
Begin each day with no forethought or preparation

*You find that you have peace of mind
and can enjoy yourself, get more
sleep, and rest when you know that it
was a one hundred percent effort
that you gave - win or lose.*

Gordie Howe
Former professional hockey player

How do I do what's best for the organization?

The difference between
try and triumph is a little <u>umph</u>.
Unknown

How do I do what's best for the organization?

Leaders who DO everyday leadership persevere and maintain personal balance in spite of challenges and difficulties. They demonstrate their personal commitment to the needs of the key stakeholders: employees, customer, organization and the community. Their leadership strength is measured in emotional and mental lifting as they strive to do what's best for the organization.

How do I do what's best for the organization?

DO	DON'T
30. Face up to issues and deal with them	30. Walk away and avoid issues
31. Fight for doing the right thing – if you know about it, you are responsible for it	31. Keep your mouth shut
32. Put the organization and its people first	32. Put yourself first, "not my problem, not my job"
33. Accept "this is our assignment" and work to make it succeed	33. Say "I don't agree with this, but I've been told we have to do it"
34. Get the right people involved and on the same page	34. Make all the decisions and define all necessary actions
35. Work with key stakeholders and other resources (e.g., departments, people)	35. Operate in a silo

How do I do what's best for the organization?

DO 30:
Face up to issues and deal with them

Why? The easy issues will get resolved. The tough issues, when managed, will cause you less pain.

What's the DO attitude? Most issues don't go away on their own, and many get worse over time. When you deal with the tough issues, you set the right example and meet your people's expectations of a dependable leader.

Why is this hard to DO? People rarely appreciate your efforts, and the issue may not be resolved quickly. Plus, you may feel over your head or afraid to take the risk.

What's the DO reward? Issues will be permanently resolved and you'll earn employees' respect for directly dealing with difficult issues.

CAUTION! Make sure you have all the facts before tackling an issue. Don't let emotion negatively affect your judgment. Recognize that well-handled emotion can improve your judgment in some situations.

- Ask: What might happen if I don't deal with this? What will happen in a week, month or year?

- Remember: "You reap what you sow"—deal with issues early and squash rumors by being fact-based and addressing assumptions.

- Manage the issue from problem to final solution—use the 50 DOs worksheet on page 13.

- Hold all people accountable for all expectations all the time (e.g., If an employee outside your manufacturing area is not wearing his protective eye gear, you should hold him accountable just as you would someone on your own team.).

- Use a calm and measured voice to handle issues—give your team the direction they need to resolve the issue (e.g., "We'll brainstorm possible solutions and narrow the list by consensus.").

- Your success:

Connected DOs:
21—Focus your efforts—pick your issues and your time
22—Defuse situations and deal with people one-on-one
36—Work through issues <u>with</u> people; listen first, then discuss
49—Contain problems and identify permanent fixes

DON'T 30:
Walk away and avoid issues

How do I do what's best for the organization?

DO 31:
Fight for doing the right thing—if you know about it, you are responsible for it

Why? Responsibility builds your credibility. When you avoid problems, they always come back to haunt you and the organization.

What does "if you know about it, you are responsible for it" mean? When you know about an issue, you must make sure the right person addresses and resolves it even if it's not within your scope of responsibility. Remember…the organization's success is everyone's success and, equally, the organization's failure is a failure for everyone.

What's the DO attitude? A common mindset is to keep your mouth shut because: "If I'm not responsible for it, I don't know about it." This DO is the opposite: "If you know about it, you <u>are</u> responsible for it." The difference is important because:
(1) Organizations need all eyes and ears open to be successful;
(2) You'll support an attitude of serving others and covering their backs; and
(3) When you see a problem, often people know you know. Your silence gives them permission to continue to do what's wrong, and you undermine your integrity and authority.

Why is this hard to DO? Risk—some people may think you are fault-finding, judgmental or interfering where you don't belong.

What's the DO reward? A better night's sleep. You won't fear going to court to defend your actions or inactions.

CAUTION! You can't do it all! Hold others accountable. Ask for help.

MORE CAUTION! Everything is not a fight! Focus your efforts on the issues critical to the organization's success.

- Understand what the "right" things are (e.g., consider short- and long-term impact on morale, costs, reputation, goals).

- List the "right things" for your team (e.g., safety rules, ethics); plan how you will hold each person accountable for these "right things"—create a "What If" game plan on paper, such as: What if an employee is caught without safety glasses? How will I respond? What are his consequences? What if someone takes home computer files without permission? What will I do?

- Lead like *you* own the company. What would you do about the situation as an owner or partner? How would you do things differently if every dime the company lost came from your check?

- Adopt "the buck stops here" as your motto. Accept responsibility for what you can manage, control or influence.

- Use the proper channels to follow up on what you see and hear—give feedback directly to the person who needs to hear it and keep others who need to know informed.

- Meet one-on-one with people who can't or won't speak up in a group setting; this will build their confidence, and you will get the benefit of their input.

- Your success:

Connected DOs:
19—Ask for help
20—Choose your own behavior; demonstrate a positive attitude and work to influence others
24—Step into a job with intensity for success – do what you can to makes things better

DON'T 31:
Keep your mouth shut

How do I do what's best for the organization?

DO 32:
Put the organization and its people first

Why? Our actions influence others' actions. Doing the right thing encourages others to do the same; everyone wins.

What's the DO attitude? An organization is usually strongly interconnected—hidden in the day-to-day details is the reality that either everyone wins or everyone loses. If you put yourself and your department first, eventually you'll hurt the organization and sabotage your own success. In the long run, the smartest thing you can do for yourself is to do what is best for the organization and its people.

Why is this hard to DO? What's best for the organization may not be obvious, it may have a negative impact on your job and/or it may be hard to do (e.g., laying off a good employee).

What's the DO reward? When the organization's goals are met or exceeded, all stakeholders benefit—you, your team and the organization.

CAUTION! To be supportive of others doesn't mean doing their jobs for them. Instead, do the best you can in a way that helps others be successful—great communication, quality hand-offs, shared resources and cross-functional problem-solving.

MORE CAUTION! If you try to do it all, you'll get burned out—both you and the organization will suffer. Do your best, then go home and enjoy the other parts of your life.

- Write your organizational, departmental or team's goals on a 3"x5" card; post the card at your desk or carry it with you as a reminder of where to focus your work; make sure your team also knows the priorities and goals.

- Help people understand how they fit into the organization, who they impact and how they impact others.

- Eliminate the phrases: "Not my problem" and "Not my job;" instead use "I'll check" and then follow up with your team.

- Focus on the quality of hand-offs: Is the information exchanged (e.g., between shifts at the plant, security guards changing posts, job-share workers and among team members) cooperative, clear, concise and constructive?

- When you deal with issues, you must think of solutions in terms of the organization's broader vision. Use a stakeholder map to help identify the people who have an investment in the outputs of a project or a decision. Ask them what they want and work to meet their needs, but do not try to do their job for them.

- Your success:

Connected DOs:
3—Lead by example—hold yourself to a higher standard
21—Focus your efforts—pick your issues and your time
24—Step into a job with intensity for success—do what you can to make things better

DON'T 32:
Put yourself first,
"not my problem, not my job"

How do I do what's best for the organization?

DO 33:
Accept "this is our assignment" and work to make it succeed

Why? Your commitment impacts how your team will support and carry out an assignment.

What does "accept this is our assignment" mean? Understand that you might not always agree with an organizational decision, but you must be 100% committed to making the organization succeed.

What's the DO attitude? Commitment is a key to success. Without your commitment:

- Poor execution wastes time and energy;
- Employees' morale is damaged by time wasted and bad results;
- People don't learn how to do their jobs better;
- Integrity and trust throughout the organization are compromised.

Why is this hard to DO? You won't agree with all the decisions you are asked to execute.

What's the DO reward? A three-way win for you, your team and the organization.

CAUTION! Don't agree to support a decision that goes against your moral or ethical values or that is clearly not in the organization's best interests. You'll regret it later!

MORE CAUTION! Don't say to your team, "We have to do this because my boss said so." This is an excuse and it doesn't add value to you or your team. Instead, take ownership for the results.

- Get clarity with the person who assigned the task; "push upwards for clarity, don't whine downwards"—ask questions to fully understand the assigned work, such as:

  * Why are we doing this?
  * What do we really want to achieve?
  * When we're done, what will it look like?

- Write down and practice "what to say instead"—rehearse positive responses, such as:

  * "This assignment supports our company goal of..."
  * "With a 10% cost savings, we'll all get larger bonuses..."
  * "The new technology keeps us ahead of competitors..."

- Model doing difficult or unpleasant tasks—lead by example.

- Your success:

Connected DOs:
18—Stay open-minded when receiving feedback
20—Choose your own behavior, demonstrate a positive attitude and work to influence others
36— Work through issues <u>with</u> people; listen first, then discuss
37—Explain why or how decisions are made

DON'T 33:
Say "I don't agree with this, but I've been told we have to do it"

How do I do what's best for the organization?

DO 34:
Get the right people involved
and on the same page

Why? You save time in the long run and make well-informed decisions.

Who are the "right people?" People who have a vested interest in a project or task, as well as the necessary skills and experience.

What's the DO attitude? Use synergy to find the right people:

- Involve stakeholders who have important project roles;
- Maximize interactions with a facilitator and small groups;
- Encourage individual strengths and involve people based on what they do well;
- Use the word *and* not *but* to build on each other's ideas; *and* promotes idea generation and limits useless debate.

Why is this hard to DO? You may not know who the "right people" are. More people means more discussion and probably more time at the front end of a project.

What's the DO reward? You will have buy-in from your people and the information you need to make a quality decision.

CAUTION! Leaving people out—those who are not considered the "right people"—can potentially cause conflict and a lack of commitment to decisions.

- Understand that people take in, process and share information
  differently; what strengths do you need on your team?
  Examples:

  * planner vs. doer
  * big picture vs. detail
  * process focus vs. task focus
  * problem focus vs. solution focus

- Adopt a common picture of success for all team members
  (e.g., focus, goals, deadlines), and write down how each
  person specifically contributes to that success.

- Plan a "no chairs" brief, information-sharing meeting where
  each person stands; this promotes involvement, energy and
  quick thinking.

- Include "non-traditional" stakeholders in the discussion
  process (e.g., suppliers, support functions, predecessors).

- Your success:

_____

_____

Connected DOs:
7—Circle back to interested parties—with follow-up, feedback,
information or an answer
11—Know who your people are, their qualifications, jobs and
where they are located
19—Ask for help

DON'T 34:
Make all the decisions and
define all necessary actions

How do I do what's best for the organization?

DO 35:
Work with key stakeholders and other resources (e.g., departments, people)

Why? Value-added work is not created in silos. (A silo is working solely within your own team or department and not across or with other teams or departments.) You are connected, interdependent, and your success requires you to work across the boundaries that silos create.

What are "key stakeholders?" People and/or groups that directly impact a team's success and need to be aligned.

What's the DO attitude? Relationships. Take the time necessary—regular phone calls, face-to-face meetings, emails—to get to know stakeholders on a more personal level.

Why is this hard to DO? Many organizations are organized, measured and rewarded by department or team, creating a silo mentality. It may seem easier, less time consuming and less frustrating to work within your own department because you have a similar agenda and goals, direct access to the people and stronger relationships.

What's the DO reward? You recognize the connectedness of your success and leverage the resources necessary to get you there. You support others and they support you.

CAUTION! Creating connections will not happen overnight! You must actively and consciously reach out and focus on mutual goals and interests.

- Identify and list people connected to a project or decision; think of the connections as the right people sitting around the table.
    * Who is impacted by the project or decisions?
    * Who will do the work to make it a success?

- Engage stakeholders and ask what their WIIFMs? (What's In It for Me?) are to understand what they need.

- Create opportunities for stakeholders to interact; schedule a social lunch or after-hours event.

- See and be seen—work with people in their cubicles, in other departments, on the production floor and in the field.

- Virtual teams (e.g., team members connected by technology and not a physical location) can use Internet and intranet forums to create quality interactions and achieve mutual understanding.

- Your success:

Connected DOs:
7—Circle back to interested parties—with follow-up, feedback, information or an answer
16—Solicit ideas from others to shape decisions
19—Ask for help
37—Explain why or how decisions are made

DON'T 35:
Operate in a silo

The ultimate measure of a man is not where he stands in moments of comfort and convenience, but where he stands at times of challenge and controversy.
Martin Luther King, Jr.
Pastor, civil rights leader and Nobel Prize recipient

How do I reduce misunderstandings and get people on the same page?

Most conversations are simply monologues delivered in the presence of witnesses.
Margaret Millar
U.S.-Canadian mystery and suspense writer

How do I reduce misunderstandings and get people on the same page?

Leaders who DO everyday leadership practice mutual understanding, resolve disputes and help others manage conflict when they see conflict as an opportunity and not as a roadblock.

How do I reduce misunderstandings and get people on the same page?

DO	DON'T
36. Work through issues <u>with</u> people; listen first, then discuss	36. Use authority first or too quickly
37. Explain why or how decisions are made	37. Say "I don't want to hear it; just do it"
38. Listen and understand first, then act	38. Make snap judgments
39. Repeat back a summary of what people have told you	39. Assume mutual understanding
40. Be completely clear about your follow-up – what you will do and won't do	40. Create false expectations because you weren't clear
41. Start meetings with rules and boundaries for discussion	41. Let discussions get out of control

How do I reduce misunderstandings and get people on the same page?

DO 36:
Work through issues <u>with</u> people; listen first, then discuss

Why? Employees have the best pulse on the day-to-day issues in their jobs and can work through most problems with guidance.

What's the DO attitude? When you use authority, you demand submission. While there are times when authority is needed, using it first or quickly puts most people into a submissive role. Over time, they'll become passive, and all issues will come to you. You'll get in over your head, feel stressed and be less productive.

To maximize success, you need everyone's hard work, input, intelligence and initiative. You build this when you work *with* people—listening, discussing and solving issues together.

Why is this hard to DO? You give up control. It's often easier and faster to share your opinion or tell people what to do without listening first.

What's the DO reward? You'll reinforce ownership of issues and develop creative solutions. You'll show your team members you respect them.

CAUTION! People may confuse listening with agreement; you need to listen, and then be clear about your decisions—what you will and won't do.

- Make good eye contact and fully listen to the person speaking.

- After listening, collect your thoughts; then check for understanding by using a phrase like, "Here's what I heard you say…" (see page 39 for more details about the ICUC™ tool of communication).

- Ask at least three open-ended questions *before* you give your point of view (see DO 44).

- Practice BrainBuilding™ (see page 125) to reinforce listening first.

- When an employee brings an issue to you, ask him if he's tried to solve the problem on his own and how that went. Look for ways to support him in the process. Develop a repertoire of engaging questions or statements such as the following:

  - "What do you think we should do?"
  - "This is your work area. What are your recommendations?"
  - "What do you want from me? How can I help you…?"
  - "Help me understand the situation…"
  - "Let's look at our options…"

- Your success:

Connected DOs:
23—Focus on the issue and not the person: "I'm not mad at you, but this behavior is unacceptable because…"
44—Ask open-ended questions
48—Be open—listen to feedback from people

DON'T 36:
Use authority first or too quickly

BrainBuilding™

Use two simple steps to support understanding among team members and stakeholders:

1. A person shares his perspective or opinion on the defined topic.

2. Each additional person first summarizes the last person's perspective, checks for understanding, then shares her perspective or opinion.

Example

The meeting topic is: Brainstorm ideas to save money on office supplies and work processes.

Kent: "Let's see if we can get volume discounts on office supplies by buying in bulk and distributing to our three work sites."

Rosa: "Kent thinks we should buy our supplies in bulk and then deliver to each work site. Is that right, Kent?"

Kent: "Yes."

Rosa: "I think we should combine payroll at each of the sites and centrally locate it to save money."

Tara: "Rosa wants to consolidate payroll to one location. Did I understand your idea correctly?"

Rosa: "Yes, you've got it!"

Tara: "Let's try to work four ten-hour days and close on Fridays."

Bradford: "Tara would like to close one day each week to save money. Is that right, Tara?"

Just being available and attentive is a great way to use listening as a management tool. Some employees will come in, talk for twenty minutes and leave having solved their problems entirely by themselves.

Nicholas V. Luppa
Author

How do I reduce misunderstandings and get people on the same page?

DO 37:
Explain why or how decisions are made

Why? Employees will learn more about the organization's goals and decision-making processes. They will feel more connected, often take greater ownership in their roles and spend less time guessing about what's going on.

What's the DO attitude? If you want people to think, to use their judgment, to take initiative and to care like business owners, then you must equip them with the bigger picture and the *why* behind decisions. Without enough information, people will naturally form their own conclusions, which will often be wrong.

If you respond to others with, "I don't want to hear it, just do it," your message is loud and clear, "I don't want you to think and I don't want you to care."

Why is this hard to DO? You must understand the *why* behind each decision. You may get questions you are not prepared to or cannot answer.

What's the DO reward? Team members will have the truth and be less likely to start rumors or waste time discussing what might be happening. They will also have a big picture perspective.

CAUTION! Give the right amount of detail! Too much detail can be overwhelming; with too little detail, people will fill in their own ideas, perceptions, interpretations and fears.

- Identify the WIIFM? (What's In It for Me?) for your team members—What do they have to gain from this decision?

- Manage anxieties by sharing enough information. Without information, people usually fill the information gap negatively, creating rumors, gossip and unnecessary anxiety.

- Explain the employee's contribution in supporting the company's decision (e.g., "You give the first impression of our company to the customer, so we need you to follow our new employee dress code.").

- Model openness...be as open as you can be with your people—tell them when you *can* tell them (e.g., "I can share with you this information about our new capital project."); and tell them when you *can't* tell them (e.g., "I can't tell you about the changes in executive leadership because of legal issues.").

- Your success:

Connected DOs:
1—Be consistently 100% honest
33—Accept "this is our assignment" and work to make it succeed
35—Work with key stakeholders and other resources (e.g., departments, people)

DON'T 37:
Say "I don't want to hear it; just do it"

How do I reduce misunderstandings and get people on
the same page?

DO 38:
Listen and understand first, then act

Why? You'll have enough information to make a quality decision.

What's the DO attitude? The power of leadership is not in how
many decisions you make or how quickly you make them. See
your people as experts—those who deal with their issues day in
and day out. Ask them to give you the details you need to take
action.

Why is this hard to DO? Time. It's hard work to be a great
listener.

What's the DO reward? You will positively involve your people
and have the necessary information to tackle an issue.

CAUTION! Don't spend all your time listening and asking
questions. Understand your time constraints—how much time you
have to make a decision—then gather information, decide and go.

MORE CAUTION! People will often assume listening to their
ideas means (1) you agree with their perspective and (2) you will
act on it. You must directly say what you understood, what you
agree with and disagree with, what your decision is and why you
made that decision.

- Ask the listener for mutual understanding by summarizing
  what you heard (see DO 39).

- Plan the time needed to gather information and multiple opinions to make the best decisions (e.g., "Let's regroup in one week, and I'll have information to share from our counterparts in the medical division.").

- Practice BrainBuilding™ (see page 125).

- Praise and reinforce those who give you good input, opinions and feedback.

- Sometimes you have to make a quick judgment. Afterwards, review the situation and figure out the lessons learned.

- Your success:

_____

_____

Connected DOs:
43—Ask people, "take me...show me"
44—Ask open-ended questions
48—Be open—listen to feedback from people

DON'T 38:
Make snap judgments

How do I reduce misunderstandings and get people on the same page?

DO 39:
Repeat back a summary of what people have told you

Why? You'll save time and energy with a mutual understanding of information.

What's the DO attitude? A commitment to establish mutual understanding between you and your people for the vision, expectations, data, decisions, plans and ideas.

Why is this hard to DO? You might feel like you're wasting time. Repeating back a summary can seem awkward at first.

What's the DO reward? You share the same picture of ideas, information, expectations and next steps.

CAUTION! You shouldn't restate word-for-word what has been said to you. Instead, use your own words to see if your understanding matches the speaker's understanding.

- Restate what you heard using phrases such as:

  * "I want to make sure I fully understood you…"
  * "Here's what I heard you say…"
  * "I sense that…"
  * "See if I got this right…"

- Check for answers to: What, when, where, why and how?

- Ask for a summary from others:

  * "What are you taking away from this discussion…?"
  * "To make sure we are on the same page, please give me a summary of what we just talked about…"

- Your summary should reflect both what you saw and what you heard. Listen to *both* the verbal and nonverbal information being shared; does the body language match the message? For example, during a performance review, does your employee have a frown on her face when she says she's "delighted" with her job?

- Check for feedback on how well you closed the loop (see page 133).

- Your success:

Connected DOs:
16—Solicit ideas from others to shape decisions
18—Stay open-minded when receiving feedback
23—Focus on the issue and not the person: "I'm not mad at you, but this behavior is unacceptable because…"
35—Work with key stakeholders and other resources (e.g., departments, people)
44—Ask open-ended questions

DON'T 39:
Assume mutual understanding

Close the Loop

There are two basic steps in communication. Step one is Send and Receive. Step two is Close the Loop. These steps are described below:

1. **Send and Receive.** This is how you would usually define "having communicated something." Jeff shares some information with Jane. Jeff assumes that Jane heard it and interprets it the same way he does. Since this first step may create a potential gap between what Jeff said and what Jane heard, Jane wonders: "Did he say what I think he said?" So...

2. **Close the Loop.** The person hearing information summarizes her understanding and the context. Jane is essentially "sharing the picture in her head," so they can check that they "see" the same thing.

Example

Jeff: "I'm going to Boise next week."

Jane: "You're going to Boise next week? This means you'll miss our staff meeting."

Jeff: "No, I won't miss the staff meeting because I'll be back by Thursday morning."

No man ever listened himself out of a job.
Calvin Coolidge
Former U.S. President

How do I reduce misunderstandings and get people on
the same page?

DO 40:
Be completely clear about your follow-up—
what you will do and won't do

Why? You'll meet others' expectations while you minimize
misunderstandings.

What is "follow-up?" Doing what you agreed to do.

What's the DO attitude? Be as clear as possible. Without clarity,
people will fill in the blanks based on their own wishes,
assumptions and prejudices, setting you up for conflict, frustration
and a lack of trust.

Why is this hard to DO? You must be specific up front about
what you will and won't do. It might be easier to think more
broadly and less about the specifics. Or you might not want to
admit that you don't have time to do something.

What's the DO reward? Team members will know they can
count on you.

CAUTION! If your organization rewards "yes" people—those
who always volunteer to take on more work—it may be hard to
say "no" to some tasks or projects.

MORE CAUTION! If you are unsure about having the time,
resources or ability to do something, speak up.

- To help organize yourself, set up a project list for what you
  will do and when you will do it; prioritize with target start and
  end dates and a priority level (e.g., urgent; important;
  whenever).

- Eliminate confusion by being specific about your expectations, such as:

  Vague and confusing: "I will complete that report."

  More clear and specific: "I will complete the Project Tree proposal next Wednesday by 3:00 p.m. I will email a copy to Barry, Conrad, Fred and Miyung."

- Ask the "scribe" in a meeting to include in the notes who has committed to what and when the task will be done (e.g., Morgan will complete a draft budget by Thursday, and Catalina will check on three alternate suppliers for hospital beds by next Tuesday.).

- Your success:

Connected DOs:
5—Commit to the extent of your knowledge and authority
21—Focus your efforts—pick your issues and your time
42—Follow through with personal commitments or come back, explain, take the pain and learn from it
45—Be honest with yourself; know what you do know and what you don't

DON'T 40:
Create false expectations
because you weren't clear

How do I reduce misunderstandings and get people on
the same page?

DO 41:
Start meetings with rules and
boundaries for discussion

Why? Poor meetings waste time and money.

What's the DO attitude? Meetings are a special kind of work and
an opportunity to uniquely multiply the knowledge, talents, skills
and experiences of individuals.

Why is this hard to DO? Discussion boundaries and rules may
seem like common sense, yet many people forget the rules when
conflict arises and emotions cloud their judgment.

What's the DO reward? You keep attendees focused on the right
results, manage conflict positively, minimize intimidation,
maximize participation and create an environment of respect and
trust.

CAUTION! This DO will take time! A long-standing team will
wonder why you are implementing new rules for their behavior.
Asking people to think and act differently may create friction.

Note: Meetings vary in size, scope and formality. Guidelines for
discussion can be used in any meeting forum, such as one-on-one,
small and large groups.

- Why are you meeting in the first place? Decide your reason(s)
  to M.E.E.T.:

  M Make a decision, a commitment to action

  E Engage creativity, new ideas and/or solutions

  E Ensure understanding, coordination, get on the same page

  T Team development, connection, ownership and enthusiasm

- Assign roles (e.g., facilitator, scribe, timekeeper, chair) for each attendee based upon strengths; allow people to try new roles with your guidance and feedback.

- Review meeting best practices at the start of a meeting (see page 139) and place them in a visible location. Merge these guidelines with your organization's core values to increase the likelihood that the best practices will be consistently used in meetings.

- Use break-out groups (e.g., pairs, triads or groups of 4 - 8 persons) to break down and discuss complex issues.

- Start with the Output required, then focus on Input and Meeting Activities. An example is:

  Output: Make a decision about 5-10 cost savings ideas in the range of $1,000 to $5,000 for XYZ Department
  Input: Invite XYZ Department stakeholders; assign a facilitator
  Meeting Activities:
  *10 minutes: Individual reflection on the Output goal
  *45 minutes: Group brainstorming
  *5 minutes: Summarize decisions and assign next steps

- Your success:

Connected DOs:
22—Defuse situations and deal with people one-on-one
23—Focus on the issue and not the person: "I'm not mad at you, but this behavior is unacceptable because..."
50—Create best practices that are standardized, documented and implemented

DON'T 41:
Let discussions get out of control

Meeting Best Practices

SET-UP

1. **MAKE SURE EVERYONE UNDERSTANDS** meeting Outputs and Best Practices

WORK

2. **START AND FINISH ON TIME**

3. **KEEP EVERYONE FOCUSED**
    - Turn off cell phones
    - Meet off-site if necessary

4. **VALUE PEOPLE'S TIME**

5. **USE FACILITATOR TO STAY ON TRACK**
    - Stay at right level of detail
    - Record off-topic issues

6. **ENSURE UNDERSTANDING**
    - Listen and take notes
    - Check for mutual understanding at each step
    - Be clear and specific

7. **BE RESPECTFUL**
    - Assume positive intent
    - One speaker at a time
    - Think before you speak
    - Build on ideas with AND not BUT

8. **ACTIVELY PARTICIPATE**
    - Say it in the meeting
    - Step up if things are getting out of hand or off-topic
    - Hold yourself and others to Meeting Best Practices

NEXT STEPS

9. **WORK TO COMMIT ON DECISIONS**
    - Minimum 70% individual agreement and
    - 100% commitment

10. **FOLLOW THROUGH ON COMMITMENTS**
    - Do them or
    - Renegotiate early—set new expectations

The real process of making decisions, of gathering support, of developing opinions, happens before the meeting or after.
Terrence E. Deal
Author

The real art of conversation is not only to say the right thing at the right place, but to leave unsaid the wrong thing at the tempting moment.
Lady Dorothy Nevill
British writer, horticulturist and hostess

How do I continue to improve what my people and I are doing?

One who asks a question is a fool for five minutes; one who does not ask a question remains a fool forever.
Chinese Proverb

How do I continue to improve what my people and I are doing?

Leaders who DO everyday leadership use life experiences—successes and failures—to develop self-awareness, take risks and make disciplined, daily changes in their attitudes and actions.

How do I continue to improve what my people and I are doing?

DO	DON'T
42. Follow through with personal commitments <u>or</u> come back, explain, take the pain and learn from it	42. Blame someone else
43. Ask people, "take me... show me"	43. Make assumptions
44. Ask open-ended questions	44. Refrain from asking questions because you think it undermines your position
45. Be honest with yourself; know what you do know and what you don't	45. Be defensive
46. Learn from others and develop tricks that work for you	46. Think there is just one way to succeed
47. Tell people up front your need to understand - task, job, process and procedures	47. Try to cover up what you don't know
48. Be open - listen to feedback from people	48. Dismiss people's feedback and ideas
49. Contain problems and identify permanent fixes	49. "Band-aid" problems – provide only "get-by" solutions
50. Create best practices that are standardized, documented and implemented	50. Lose learning by not documenting and sharing issues and solutions

How do I continue to improve what my people and I are doing?

DO 42:
Follow through with personal commitments <u>or</u> come back, explain, take the pain and learn from it

Why? People will learn to count on you. And you'll build relationships of trust, credibility and respect.

What does "take the pain" mean? Deal with the consequences of not following through and move on.

What's the DO attitude? How good is your word? Can people trust what you say? Can they put faith in you and your commitments? Daily, you prove the strength of your word by your actions. You prove your commitment by either following through or facing the consequences of not following through.

Why is this hard to DO? Sometimes factors outside your control can keep you from meeting deadlines and commitments. You may make an unrealistic commitment just to get people off your back, or you may simply make a mistake and not follow through.

What's the DO reward? People will trust you to get things done with a 100% commitment.

CAUTION! A pattern of too many explanations and deadline extensions, no matter how sincere, will eventually undermine your credibility: "He has good intentions but he just doesn't deliver."

- Evaluate why you are not following through: Do you take on too much and need to set boundaries? Do you avoid some work? Do you need to practice saying "no?"

- Make an apology if you goof, misjudge or don't follow through and build in concrete steps to make sure it doesn't happen again (use FACET™ tool for positive change, on page 63 or downloadable at www.humanergy.com).

- Think of your commitments as a *guarantee* that your work will get done. Track your commitments to remind you of your daily guarantees.

- When a project deadline is near and you know you won't be able to meet it, as soon as possible, renegotiate the due date or timeline (e.g., "I need an extra week to complete the proposal for a new computer system. I'll contact the project leader and request a timeline extension.").

- Your success:

_____

_____

Connected DOs:
7—Circle back to interested parties—with follow-up, feedback, information or an answer
28—Write down thoughts, facts and issues—make lists, prioritize and check off
29—Prepare and start the day with a game plan—to dos
40—Be completely clear about your follow-up—what you will do and won't do

DON'T 42:
Blame someone else

How do I continue to improve what my people and I are doing?

DO 43:
Ask people, "take me...show me"

Why? Better information equals better decisions.

What does "take me...show me" mean? Ask employees to show you what's happening (e.g., a glitch in the computer program, a jam in the conveyor belt, inconsistent shipping invoices); there's no substitute for first-hand knowledge.

What's the DO attitude? Verbal and written reports are filtered through people's world-view, self-deception, and what they think you want to hear. Seeing what's happening firsthand is worth a thousand reports. By comparing and contrasting your observation with what people tell you, you can evaluate their objectivity and judgment.

Why is this hard to DO? Time, the ability to listen well and an open mind.

What's the DO reward? You will be better informed.

CAUTION! "Take me...show me" time could easily fill your entire work day! Balance "take me...show me" with your other priorities.

- Lead with the learning attitude. Approach each situation with the questions: "What can he teach me?" AND "What can I teach him?"

- **ASK** questions = <u>A</u>lways <u>S</u>eek <u>K</u>nowledge: Practice DO 44!

- List and practice "ask for help" phrases such as:

    * "I don't know much about..."
    * "I'm here to learn..."
    * "Let's work together to use all the knowledge here..."

- Create a workplace model for interactive problem-solving conversations (e.g., use plastic toy building blocks to mimic the actual production layout or a job board to coordinate jobs and available people).

- Your success:

_____

_____

Connected DOs:
2—Say "I don't know; I'll find out"
9—Trust people and check their work when necessary
13—Spend time side-by-side with people
19—Ask for help

DON'T 43:
Make assumptions

How do I continue to improve what my people and I are doing?

DO 44:
Ask open-ended questions

Why? You will learn, understand and achieve more.

What's an "open-ended" question? A question that cannot be answered with a simple "yes," "no" or "maybe." Example: "What three things can we do to improve our relationship with the community?" OR "How would you propose we cut $2 million from the capital budget?"

What's the DO attitude? Be willing to admit to yourself and others that you don't know everything. Create an atmosphere that encourages everyone to question and learn, so that your team's abilities are maximized.

Why is this hard to DO? Asking great questions requires time, sincerity and the ability to fully listen. It requires admitting you don't know everything.

What's the DO reward? Your team will work harder and be more loyal when they know you want their input and value their ideas, and you'll be smarter!

CAUTION! Don't dilute the power of a great question by not giving people time to think about their responses.

- Set aside time each day to be a "questioner;" suspend your thinking, knowledge and judgment to make certain you really understand others' ideas.

- Ask at least three probing, open-ended questions *before* you give your point of view; an example follows.

  > Team Member: "We have a conveyor belt problem."
  > **Leader:** "Tell me about it."
  > Team Member: "It made a screeching noise about midway through the shift."
  > **Leader:** "What do you think is going on?"
  > Team Member: "It is the same thing we fixed last week."
  > **Leader:** "What do you recommend...?"

- Keep a Learning Log—when you ask a question and learn something, record what you've learned; use the log as a reference to avoid repeating mistakes and keep learning as your focus.

- Your success:

Connected DOs:
2—Say "I don't know; I'll find out"
16—Solicit ideas from others to shape decisions
19—Ask for help
38—Listen and understand first, then act

DON'T 44:
Refrain from asking questions because you think it undermines your position

How do I continue to improve what my people and I are doing?

DO 45:
Be honest with yourself; know what you do know and what you don't

Why? When you recognize and acknowledge your own limits, your people will see you as an authentic leader.

What does "be honest with yourself" mean? Self awareness—taking the time to understand your strengths, weaknesses and the perceptions others have of you.

What's the DO attitude? When people become aware of a performance weakness, they often go through a process similar to grieving. Use the four steps of **SARA** (**S**hock, **A**nger, **R**ejection and **A**cceptance) to help you digest your weaknesses. Then create a strategy for change (see FACET™, page 63).

Why is this hard to DO? Pride. Being wrong, not knowing or not being good at something can be uncomfortable. It can also be painful when someone points it out.

What's the DO reward? You will grow as a person and a leader.

CAUTION! Be realistic in your expectations and don't be too hard on yourself. Give yourself time to process constructive feedback.

- List your skills and knowledge; rate each strength and use this as a guide for making commitments, such as this example:
    * Customer service protocol—excellent
    * Computer skills (word processing, spreadsheets)—excellent
    * Company policies—good
    * Balance sheet basics—good
    * Marketing strategy—fair

- Pick one area of your skills and knowledge to improve; use the FACET™ tool on page 63 to make a change; post your improvement plan.

- Prepare yourself for criticism by reminding yourself that you can always improve; feedback is a gift.

- Ask a peer to tell you about any emotional or defensive reactions you might have.

- Ask questions—allow your team members to give you honest input, train you about the specifics of their jobs and give insights unique to their roles in the organization.

- Schedule quarterly informal meetings with your team members and ask, What do I do well? Where can I improve?

- Biannually, ask your boss, team and peers for formal feedback to assess your strengths and improvement areas.

- Your success:

Connected DOs:
1—Be consistently 100% honest
5—Commit to the extent of your knowledge and authority
16—Solicit ideas from others to shape decisions
19—Ask for help
35—Work with key stakeholders and other resources (e.g., departments, people)

DON'T 45:
Be defensive

How do I continue to improve what my people and I are doing?

DO 46:
Learn from others and develop tricks that work for you

Why? You will be open-minded to new ideas and grow as a leader.

What are "tricks?" Tips, shortcuts and best practices for efficiently and effectively completing your work and leading · others.

What's the DO attitude? Don't reinvent the wheel—your challenges are not completely unique. Many people have been down this road before you. Be smart and learn from them. Pick what works for you—experiment, adapt and refine.

Why is this hard to DO? Old habits and comfort zones are hard to change. It's humbling to admit that your way may not be the best.

What's the DO reward? You will increase your learning and leading ten-fold!

CAUTION! One size does not fit all. Some tricks might work for you and some might not. Build on your own strengths, weaknesses and style rather than trying to mimic another team member. You can look to others as role models, but you need to lead your way.

MORE CAUTION! Don't try to implement too many new ideas at one time. You'll be overwhelmed!

• Your attitude is contagious. Model an excitement for learning!

- Allocate ten minutes of your team's meeting agenda to share lessons learned by individual team members; record these lessons for future reference.

- Take notes in meetings; review after the meeting and highlight what you learned.

- Identify role models—watch what they do and learn from what works.

- Publicly acknowledge team members who teach you something (e.g., at staff or team meetings, on bulletin boards, in group emails).

- Create a Learnings List for each project; write what worked and what didn't; share and compare your lists with other project teams and departments.

- Collect leadership tips from e-newsletters, business magazines and professional and trade journals; use what works for you and pass along tips to co-workers.

- Your success:

Connected DOs:
2—Say "I don't know; I'll find out"
16—Solicit ideas from others to shape decisions
35—Work with key stakeholders and other resources (e.g., departments, people)
50—Create best practices that are standardized, documented and implemented

DON'T 46:
Think there is just one way to succeed

How do I continue to improve what my people and I are doing?

DO 47:
Tell people up front your need to understand— task, job, process and procedures

Why? You'll be an effective leader and model for information sharing and free flow of ideas.

What's the DO attitude? A common mindset is knowledge equals competence. A better mindset is that competence is measured by what you deliver. You need information to be successful, so getting it early creates competence. Don't fall into the trap of covering up what you don't know—people will find out, and your credibility will be damaged.

Why is this hard to DO? Humility. You'll have to admit you don't know everything!

What's the DO reward? You'll get the information you need and demonstrate your competence.

CAUTION! Ask for the right level of detail. Don't let too many details bog you down and keep you from making progress.

- Tell direct reports that you need to know the specifics about what they do, and ask them to be a partner in educating you.

- Set expectations of how you want information given to you; provide a template with necessary details (e.g., date, time, cost per item, number ordered, total cost).

- Ask your boss to give you the same information when she assigns you a project: What's the project outcome? What's the deadline? Who are the key stakeholders? What are their WIIFMs (What's In It For Me?)?

- Your success:

_____

_____

Connected DOs:
2—Say "I don't know; I'll find out"
9—Trust people and check their work when necessary
19—Ask for help
25—Collect the information needed for any given task from your people

DON'T 47:
Try to cover up what you don't know

How do I continue to improve what my people and I are doing?

DO 48:
Be open—listen to feedback from people

Why? Other people's input will help you expand and refine your own understanding. You'll expand and refine the learning of your people.

What's the DO attitude? Your world is limited if you only listen to your own feedback and ideas. Even though you are talented, you don't know everything or enough to succeed by yourself.

Why is this hard to DO? It's natural to form a reply while someone is speaking instead of listening to understand. And you may need to admit you aren't always right or don't know it all.

What's the DO reward? Employees will appreciate your concern and genuine interest in their opinions. You'll get great ideas from team members who do their jobs well.

CAUTION! Don't allow gripe sessions to clog your schedule. When people recognize you as a person who will listen, they may take advantage of you!

- Set up an idea and feedback system; use a box and note cards or dedicated email address to get feedback from your team members.

- Socrates said, "Know thyself." Recognize, when it comes to hearing feedback, you may not fully understand your own attitudes and actions.

- Build in a mandatory process to evaluate lessons learned after a project is completed.

- Your success:

Connected DOs:
16—Solicit ideas from others to shape decisions
35—Work with key stakeholders and other resources (e.g., departments, people)
36—Work through issues with people; listen first, then discuss
38—Listen and understand first, then act

DON'T 48:
Dismiss people's feedback and ideas

How do I continue to improve what my people and I are doing?

DO 49:
Contain problems and
identify permanent fixes

Why? Problem "work-arounds" cause you ongoing pain. Remember: If you never have time to do it right, you'll find time to do it over!

What is a "band-aid" fix? Quick resolution to a problem that resolves it temporarily, but isn't a long-term solution.

What's the DO attitude? Think of the long view. What will the short-term fix cost us today, in a month or a year?

Why is this hard to DO? Short-term fixes are often easier, quicker and less costly. "Band-aids" make problems invisible until they creep up again.

What's the DO reward? You stop problems from getting worse, and you find solutions that focus on prevention. Long-term fixes usually cost less.

CAUTION! If you constantly work in a "crisis" or "putting out fires" mode, you are comfortable with "band-aids." It will be harder for you to think of permanent solutions.

- Reality demands a real-time response to fires or crises. Contain the problem and limit the damage and consequences; when the fire is out, follow up with the resources (budget, time and people) to fix the problem with a permanent solution.

- Create a log that identifies quick fixes, re-fixes and permanent fixes; post it publicly; review and update the log regularly and keep it accessible to your employees.

- Prioritize your permanent fixes by asking yourself and your team these questions:

  * What's going on here?
  * Are we using band-aids or are we preventing repeat issues with a permanent solution?
  * How do we make the situation better?
  * What can we do to prevent a recurrence?
  * If we use a band-aid, what are the long-term consequences of today's short-term fix?
  * What's our *first* step?

- When a permanent fix is put in place, check the issue off your "fix-it list" and reward your team.

- Use the Internet as a resource to research similar projects or issues; join a chat group that discusses your problem.

- Your success:

Connected DOs:
25—Collect the information needed for any given task from your people
30—Face up to issues and deal with them
32—Put the organization and its people first

DON'T 49:
"Band-aid" problems—
provide only "get-by" solutions

How do I continue to improve what my people and I are doing?

DO 50:
Create best practices that are standardized, documented and implemented

Why? Your success comes from a disciplined use of best practices refined by learning.

What are "best practices?" The best way to get results: A method or technique that, through experience and research, leads to a consistent, desired result.

What's the DO attitude? Model sharing and documenting new ideas and best practices. Use tricks from outside your industry and area of expertise. Reward people for using best practices, and for standardizing and documenting them.

Why is this hard to DO? It is easier to do something the way it's always been done. Organizations and people tend to repeat their negative history.

What's the DO reward? You and your team are continually achieving your results in a new and improved way while outpacing the competition.

CAUTION! Humans resist change! When you replace a current practice with a best practice or a best practice with a better practice, employees will dig in their heels as you drag them along.

- Pick one location for capturing best practices; log them by subject (e.g., people, programs, paperwork, clients) and use worksheets for tasks that are routinely repeated (e.g., payroll, production changeovers and stockholder mailings).

- Review best practices regularly; replace with *better* practices.

- Reward employees who recommend a new best practice that is then implemented by you and your team; rewards might include a company T-shirt, gift certificate to a local restaurant or cash bonus accompanied by a note of recognition.

- Build a lessons-learned review into each project or routine work practice; ask the team and your customers or end users "What worked?" and "What didn't work?" (see page 13 for the 50 DOs worksheet).

- Convert lessons learned into changes in process and procedure; communicate these changes and new expectations to the affected employees or departments.

- Your success:

_____

_____

Connected DOs:
15—Give out work assignments, document accountability and hold people accountable
28—Write down thoughts, facts and issues—make lists, prioritize and check off
46—Learn from others and develop tricks that work for you

DON'T 50:
Lose learning by not documenting and sharing issues and solutions

Got Success?

Share your 50 DOs successes and tips with us! We may use your idea in a future printing of *50 DOs for Everyday Leadership.*

Email: info@humanergy.com

Mail: Humanergy®
        50 DOs for Everyday Leadership
        213 West Mansion Street
        Marshall, MI 49068

If we decide to use your tip in a future edition of the *50 DOs for Everyday Leadership*, we will give you acknowledgement.

Important note: Sending us your submission does not ensure we will use it in any publication. Your successes, tips and ideas become property of Humanergy® and Humanergy® retains all rights.

Glossary

Best Practice—A method that, through experience and research, leads to a consistent desired result; a best way to get results

Interdependence—Connections in the workplace where one person's input is another person's output; working together is essential to achieve success

Mutual Understanding—Communication that goes the extra distance to make sure each person comprehends and knows the other's perspective

Silo—Working solely within your own team or department and not across or with other teams or departments.

Stakeholder—Key people and/or groups that are directly connected to the team's success and need to be in alignment

Stakeholder Mapping—The process of outlining the key people who have a stake in the outcome of a project

Stakeholder Success—Recognize and address the key stakeholder WIIFM? (What's In It for Me?) from his or her perspective

Supervisor—A "formal" organizational leader; a person responsible for the performance of another

Synergy—Using team members' collective viewpoints, diverse skills, learnings and educational and experiential backgrounds to create the best possible solution

Team Member—Any co-worker who is part of a team

WIIFM (What's In It For Me?)—What's the benefit for me as an individual? What can I expect from this if I go along?

Ignite your Success

What is Humanergy®?

Humanergy is people working together with energy and creativity to produce world-changing results. Our mission is to cultivate this approach within teams and companies. John Barrett and David Wheatley created the word "Humanergy" when they founded the company in the year 2000.

HUMAN + SYNERGY = HUMANERGY

We believe Humanergy® requires combining practices that are often seen as mutually exclusive—the human *Art* with the *Science* of work. The *Art* includes leadership, trust, mutual understanding, valuing differences and commitment. The *Science* includes goals, measurement, best practices, analysis, planning, and accountability.

Humanergy® provides coaching, training, facilitation and tools for the *Art* and *Science* of working together. The general areas of our work are: *Leadership, Teamwork, Communication and Organizational Development.*

Bring Humanergy® Trainings to your Organization

Humanergy® is committed to providing training that:

◊   Targets real performance needs
◊   Results in improved performance (thinking and behavior)
◊   Builds on what is working and does not waste resources
◊   Uses the best approach to get the desired results

The following four-hour training programs will be tailored to you and your organization's specific needs:

50 DOs for Everyday Leadership
Apply the 50 DOs to your organization and your particular leadership needs

Meeting 1, 2, 3: Fewer, More Productive Meetings
Focus on your outcomes first, then the necessary inputs and process to get you there

DESIRED™ Results: Coaching and Delegation with Real Accountability
A seven-step process to ensure consistent performance standards

Mutual Understanding: Clear Speaking and Complete Listening
Ensure that people understand others' perspectives

Humanergy® Trainings *(continued)*

TrueSuccess™: Focus Action for the Right Results
Disciplined thinking for proactive, interdependent and strategic direction

Synergy: Make Differences Work to your Advantage
Use different perspectives to create the best direction

Commitment: Get Buy-in and Stay-in
Gain everyone's emotional buy-in to the direction

Integrity: Walk the Talk
Follow through on commitments

Leadership: Transform Thinking and Behavior
Promote discipline, focus and direction

We also offer executive and team *coaching*, expert *facilitation* of strategic and difficult work sessions, *experiential team building* and thirty to sixty-minute leadership *keynotes*.

For more information contact Humanergy® at 269.789.0446 or info@humanergy.com.

Visit us on the web at: www.humanergy.com

About the Authors

John Barrett has dedicated more than sixteen years to coaching, facilitating and training to help individuals and organizations thrive.

John's clients describe him as authentic, integrity-based and able to provide a balance of challenge and support that accelerates change. He has a unique talent to quickly understand people, teams and organizations and create a practical approach that gets the right results.

John is a former research director with Outward Bound Australia, where he evaluated program effectiveness and led training adventures in the Australian wilderness. He received a graduate degree in psychology and math from the Australian National University.

John plays the didgeridoo, a musical instrument created from a tree trunk hollowed out by insects and unique to the Aboriginal culture in the Outback. His passions include his family and singing.

David Wheatley has devoted more than sixteen years to coaching and training individuals for professional and personal successes.

David's clients describe him as high-energy, real and with a readiness to "roll up his sleeves" and work alongside them. He has an exceptional ability to assess clients' needs, customize accordingly and move them forward.

David is a former Scotland Yard officer and a graduate of the Hendon Police College in London. He is also an honors graduate of Lancaster University's education program in the United Kingdom.

David's personal passions include his family, as well as coaching and playing soccer.

About the Authors *(continued)*

Lynn Townsend has a decade of technology, manufacturing and communication experience from a Fortune 500 perspective. She is founder and president of Eternally Speaking®, a communication consulting company.

Clients appreciate her down-to-earth wisdom, quick wit and practical ideas for improving team and personal communication.

Lynn has a bachelor's degree in Food Science from Purdue University and a master's in Organizational Communication from Western Michigan University. She is an award-winning writer, motivational speaker and inspirational vocalist.

Lynn's personal passions include her family, faith, music and learning for life.

Index

Index

Index

Index

Index

ORDER FORM

Have questions? Need help? Call 269.789.0446
To order online, visit us at www.humanergy.com or www.50DOs.com

Please send me more copies of the *50 DOs for Everyday Leadership* book
1-15 copies: $16.95   16-50 copies: $14.95   51+ copies: $12.95

Books   Number of books _____ x Price (see above) =$ _____
Additional Resources
50 DOs/DON'Ts Laminated Job Aid Card _____ copies x $10.00 =$ _____
Meeting Best Practices Poster _____ copies x $75.00 =$_____
Meeting Best Practices Tabletop Card _____ copies x $10.00 =$_____

Product Total $ _____
*Shipping/Handling $ _____
Subtotal $ _____
Sales Tax— 6% (MI only) $ _____
TOTAL (U.S. dollars only) $ _____

Prices effective December 1, 2006 and are subject to change.

*Shipping & Handling Charges

Total $ Amount	Up to $25	$26-$49	$50-$99	$100-$249	$250-$1200	$1201 & up
Total Shipping	$4	$6	$9	$16	$30	FREE

Call 269.789.0446 for orders to be shipped outside continental U.S.
Orders shipped ground delivery; 6-8 business days

Name _____Title_____
Organization_____
Shipping Address (no P.O. Boxes)_____
_____
City _____ State _____ Zip_____
Phone _____FAX_____
Email_____
- Charge your order:___ MasterCard ___ Visa ___ Amer. Express
- Credit Card No. _____ Exp. _____
- Cardholder's Name _____
- Check Enclosed (payable to: HUMANERGY)
- Please Invoice (orders over $300 only) P.O.#_____

Fax	**Mail**	**Phone**
269.789.0057	213 West Mansion Marshall, MI 49068	269.789.0446